CONFRONTING SUBURBAN POVERTY IN AMERICA

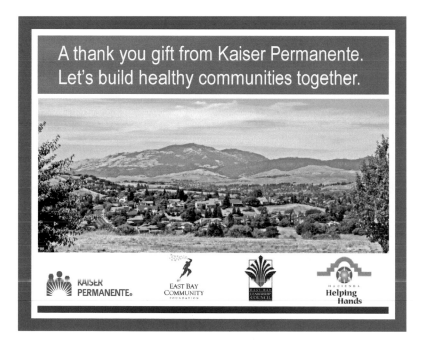

A thank you gift from Kaiser Permanente. Let's build healthy communities together.

KAISER PERMANENTE.

EAST BAY COMMUNITY FOUNDATION

EAST BAY LEADERSHIP COUNCIL

HACIENDA Helping Hands

CONFRONTING SUBURBAN POVERTY IN AMERICA

Elizabeth Kneebone

Alan Berube

Brookings Institution Press
Washington, D.C.

The Library of Congress has cataloged the hardcover editon as follows:
Kneebone, Elizabeth.
    Confronting suburban poverty in America / Elizabeth Kneebone and Alan Berube.
        pages   cm
    Includes bibliographical references and index.
    ISBN 978-0-8157-2390-5 (hardcover : alk. paper)
    1. Poor—Government policy—United States. 2. Poor—United States. 3. Suburbs—
United States—Economic conditions. I. Berube, Alan. II. Title.
    HV95.K57 2013
    362.5'560973091733—dc23   2013009767
            ISBN 978-0-8157-2580-0 (pbk. : alk. paper)

Digital printing

Printed on acid-free paper

Typeset in Sabon

Composition by Peter Lindeman
Arlington, Virginia

Contents

Foreword

In January 1964 President Lyndon Johnson spoke to Congress and the American people to announce that the United States was declaring a war against poverty: "It will not be a short or easy struggle," said Johnson. "No single weapon or strategy will suffice, but we shall not rest until that war is won. The richest Nation on earth can afford to win it. We cannot afford to lose it."

What came next were a set of ambitious initiatives, from Head Start and Job Corps to Vista and a host of other antipoverty programs. As a boy growing up in the South Bronx, raised by a working mother who made $50 a week, living in a tenement surrounded by what were at the time the most dangerous streets in America, I was offered real hope for a better life by these programs. That was fifty years ago.

Today, the War on Poverty is out of the national consciousness, but the deep-rooted inequities it attempted to ameliorate are still very much with us. Worse, the continued economic bifurcation of our society has too often pushed poverty beyond our sight. The geography of poverty and opportunity in the United States looks strikingly different. The majority of the metropolitan poor now live outside cities, and the suburban poor are the fastest-growing low-income population in the country.

As Elizabeth Kneebone and Alan Berube have painstakingly documented in *Confronting Suburban Poverty in America*, there are today poor families in suburban communities such as Seat Pleasant, Maryland; Edgewater, Colorado; and Mount Vernon, New York, facing many of the same challenges that I faced decades ago in the South Bronx.

American suburbs close to prospering urban centers, once the aspiration of city dwellers and the key to a better life, have now become home to the same cycles of poverty that in previous decades trapped people in the nation's bleakest urban neighborhoods. Ironically, a child growing up today in one of this nation's poorest suburban zip codes may have a more difficult path to opportunity and inclusion than we did in the

South Bronx. To be sure we attended underperforming schools, lived in substandard housing, had a dearth of good available jobs, and dealt constantly with the fear of crime. But at the same time Manhattan was then just an inexpensive subway ride away and offered us a range of economic, educational, and cultural opportunities.

That community safety net—the infrastructure that augments incomes, supplements education, and knits together health services for a plethora of families—kept many from falling deeper into poverty and despair. For some of us it became a path to a better and more contributory life. Indeed, the War on Poverty was transformational. In 1964, 19 percent of the country found itself living below the poverty line. By the end of the decade that number had dropped to 12 percent, because the lives of millions of Americans had changed in the process.

But in recent years those numbers have risen, and for poor suburban families, their challenges are compounded by lengthy and costly commutes to work, a lack of reliable public transportation, and an absence of basic health and social services that are more fully available and established in urban neighborhoods.

Very little infrastructure exists to expand opportunity among the poor in the nation's suburbs, in part because the way we think about poverty in America is dominated by stereotypes and solutions from a bygone era. That's why *Confronting Suburban Poverty in America* is such a timely and important book. Remaking the lay of the land of poverty by articulating the facts of its suburban reality, this book represents precisely the sort of clear thinking on how to address scarcity and inequality wherever they arise.

The Ford Foundation is proud to have played a seminal role in the War on Poverty. Many of the original antipoverty programs were built on ideas backed by the Ford Foundation, including the Gray Areas programs in Boston, Oakland, New Haven, Philadelphia, and Washington, D.C. Later, Ford worked closely with New York senator Robert Kennedy in seeking to bring private enterprise to America's inner cities, such as Brooklyn's Bedford-Stuyvesant neighborhood. The continued presence of Community Development Corporations in cities across this country is a lasting legacy of those efforts.

Today, Ford's commitment to expand opportunity in our country continues. In 2010 the Ford Foundation committed $200 million to a new Metropolitan Opportunity initiative, which supports integrated efforts that reach beyond individual neighborhoods to connect individuals to the full potential offered in their wider metropolitan region.

The poor, like so many of us, are drawn to regional employment opportunities, participate in metropolitan labor markets, search for homes in regional housing markets, and work in industries and services that are interdependent within close geographic proximity. This is one of the reasons we are working with the Metropolitan Policy Program at the Brookings Institution to help policymakers and the public overcome outdated perceptions of where poverty is and who it affects, with the goal of more effectively connecting low-income people to opportunity now out of reach within their regions.

This is also why I'm particularly pleased that *Confronting Suburban Poverty in America* highlights the work of our grantees such as the Metropolitan Planning Council, which is working to facilitate cooperation among suburbs on matters of mutual municipal interest, like affordable housing production; the Bay Area Transit-Oriented Affordable Housing Fund, a regional development fund that provides financing for the development of affordable housing and other vital community services near transit lines throughout the Bay Area; and the Urban Institute's Work Support Strategies, which is devising innovative ways to streamline and simplify the process by which states and counties provide a range of benefits to families. These innovators are advancing creative solutions to both entrenched and emerging problems. They offer important lessons for what a more effective and modern effort to expand opportunity and eradicate poverty can and must look like.

But, as was the case fifty years ago, today's challenge is in bringing these pioneering responses to scale. Inventing the next generation of place-based strategies to advance economic opportunity will require participation by both the public and private sectors, as well as nonprofit and philanthropic leadership and coordination. This book lays out concrete steps and an urgent call to action to create a more effective policy and practice framework that can respond to the scale and shifts of today's needs. As President Johnson reminded us in 1964, "The war on poverty must be won in the field, in every private home, in every public office, from the courthouse to the White House." *Confronting Suburban Poverty in America* gives us the road map to do just that—and to continue the struggle to make access to opportunity a reality in the life of all Americans.

Luis A. Ubiñas
President of the Ford Foundation

Acknowledgments

We first got into the issue of suburban poverty by accident. We came to the Metropolitan Policy Program to study the social issues facing cities and regions, most notably poverty, and to advance public policy that addresses them. Both of us were motivated to pursue this line of work by journalists such as Alex Kotlowitz and scholars such as William Julius Wilson who did so much to portray the urgency of the challenges facing America's inner-city neighborhoods and their residents. Other than having grown up in the suburbs like most Americans our age (Elizabeth around Indianapolis; Alan around Worcester, Massachusetts), neither of us ever really studied suburbia very carefully. And each of us today lives in a big city (Washington, D.C.).

But in 2006 we wrote a Brookings report about poverty trends in cities and metropolitan areas in the 2000s. Buried within our analysis was a trend that struck us as noteworthy: by our calculations, there now seemed to be more poor people in metro areas living outside of big cities than within them. We spoke with a lot of people about the report, and they had trouble wrapping their heads around that statistic. Admittedly, we did, too.

Not long after, we approached the Ford Foundation with the idea that this phenomenon of rapidly growing suburban poverty deserved careful analysis. What was it, why was it happening, and what did it mean? Ford generously funded Brookings's Metropolitan Opportunity series, which gave us and several of our research partners around the country the chance to explore these trends, causes, and consequences in much greater depth. The Annie E. Casey Foundation became a supporter of the series as well. We think it's fair to say that none of us grappled with this issue because we cared more about the suburban poor than the urban (or rural, for that matter) poor, but because the "suburbanization of poverty" seemed to call into question the way our society frames and addresses the issue of poverty altogether. Like so many of the other issues our colleagues work on at the Metropolitan Policy Program, it was an area that seemed overdue to "go metro."

This book represents our effort to add up what that Metro Opportunity research revealed, and to articulate what we think it implies for the future of anti-poverty policy. Perhaps most important, the process of writing the book gave us the chance to travel to regions around the country, to engage with thoughtful, highly innovative individuals and organizations who are inventing that future today, and to give their efforts the prominence they so richly deserve.

Our principal sponsor in this multiyear effort was the Ford Foundation, and particularly Don Chen in its Metro Opportunity Unit. The foundation's and Don's continued interest, financial support, and guidance for our work on this issue at Brookings were absolutely critical. We are grateful as well to the Annie E. Casey Foundation and Bob Giloth for their contributions to our efforts in this area.

The act of turning ideas into a printed reality would not have been possible without the efforts of so many wonderful colleagues at Brookings. Bruce Katz provided us with abiding, invaluable direction and support here at the Metropolitan Policy Program. Other program colleagues served as reviewers, contributors to the Metro Opportunity series, and supportive advisers along the way, including Jennifer Bradley, Jeanine Forsythe, Carrie Kolasky, Amy Liu, Mark Muro, Robert Puentes, Audrey Singer, Adie Tomer, and Jill Wilson. A veritable army of research assistants and interns made critical, substantive contributions to the book, including Mindy Ault, Megha Bansal, Greg Entwhistle, Oleg Firsen, Emily Garr, Carey Anne Nadeau, Etan Newman, and Jane Williams. And many of our other Brookings co-workers participated in occasional meetings and brown-bag sessions that made this book better by helping us to ask new questions or look at issues in different ways. We also thank the dedicated team at Brookings Institution Press for bringing all of the pieces together into this finished product, including Janet Walker who guided us through this process and helped keep us on track. Thanks as well to Barbara Ray and her colleagues at Hired Pen whose editorial assistance helped sharpen and clarify drafts of each chapter.

We are also indebted to a number of partners and collaborators outside Brookings, who have made valuable contributions to the Metro Opportunity Series over the years and informed our thinking on the factors that shape the growth in and experience of poverty in the suburbs. Kenya Covington at California State University, Northridge; Naomi Cytron at the Federal Reserve Bank of San Francisco; Lance Freeman at

Columbia University; Steven Raphael and Carolina Reid at the University of California, Berkeley; Sarah Reckhow at Michigan State University; Benjamin Roth at the University of Chicago; Chris Schildt at PolicyLink; Michael Stoll at the University of California, Los Angeles; and Roberto Suro at the University of Southern California have asked important questions about the causes and implications of suburban poverty through their research, and, in answering those questions, have provided rich and illuminating analyses on which we draw in the early chapters of this book. Scott Allard at the University of Chicago and Margaret Weir at the University of California, Berkeley, not only contributed critical research to the Metro Opportunity Series, but, along with David Erickson at the Federal Reserve Bank of San Francisco and Robin Snyderman at BRicK Partners, acted as trusted sounding boards throughout the book-writing process and provided insightful comments and questions on earlier drafts of the full manuscript.

We also benefited greatly from the guidance of practitioners and innovators from across the country. Through multiple meetings, phone calls, presentations, and reviews of draft chapters, these individuals helped us test and hone our messages, highlight innovations from a diverse set of regions and communities, and fine tune recommendations: Angela Blanchard and Roberta Achtenberg at Neighborhood Centers (which also hosted us and several partners for a daylong session in May 2012); Patrice Cromwell at the Annie E. Casey Foundation; Jeff Faulkner at Ways to Work; Lisa Davis at the Ford Foundation; Steve Goldberg at Social Finance; Bill Goldsmith at Mercy Portfolio Services; Ira Goldstein at The Reinvestment Fund; Trinita Logue and Joe Neri at IFF; Shirley Marcus Allen and Carol Thompson Cole at Venture Philanthropy Partners; David Pope, former village president of Oak Park, Ill.; Brian Prater at Low Income Investment Fund; Jim Rokakis at Thriving Communities Institute; and Paul Weech at the Housing Partnership Network.

In the end, this book is about places. Through our travels to a diverse group of regions, we were able to spend time in communities touched by growing suburban poverty and learn from local leaders and practitioners grappling with the challenges of rapidly rising need amid increasingly strained resources. A number of partners made those productive visits possible by pulling together key stakeholders, offering meeting spaces, and organizing community tours. For their generous support during our time in the Chicago region, we thank Mary Sue Barrett at the Metropolitan Planning Council and Robin Synderman and her team at BRicK Partners; in Cleveland, Emily Garr and Brad Whitehead at Fund

For Our Economic Future; in Denver, Sarah Hughes at the Colorado Children's Campaign and Lisa Piscopo at the City and County of Denver's Office of Children's Affairs; in Seattle, Joan Machlis and Mary Jean Ryan at the Road Map Project; in Pittsburgh, Alexandra Murphy at the University of Michigan; and in the San Francisco Bay area, Chris Schildt at PolicyLink and Bob Uyeki at the Y & H Soda Foundation. During our visits to these regions, we met with scores of elected officials, agency staff, researchers, social service providers, educators, and administrators who offered their perspectives on the changes taking place within their communities and the related challenges, responses, and opportunities they saw evolving in their regions. We deeply appreciate the insights these individuals shared, the questions they raised, and the practical approaches they offered to these complex issues. These conversations helped to ground our research and recommendations in the everyday reality of what it means to confront suburban poverty.

Finally, we thank our families and friends, and most especially Diana Hristova, Cristina Boccuti, and Erica Berube for their love, support, and understanding during many late-night writing and editing sessions, and for all the other moments in the day, too.

CONFRONTING
SUBURBAN POVERTY
IN AMERICA

CHAPTER **1**

Poverty and the Suburbs:
An Introduction

Drive about forty-five miles east of San Francisco, tracing a route across the Bay Bridge, through the Caldecott Tunnel outside Oakland, past the wealthy suburbs of central Contra Costa County, and along the California Delta Highway that eventually leads to the state's Central Valley. There you find a series of communities in transition—from industrial cities to bedroom suburbs, from agricultural lands to residential havens, and from outposts of the middle class to symbols of modern American poverty.

In the 2000s, the number of people living in poverty in East Contra Costa County ("East County") grew by more than 70 percent—a rapid increase for these relatively small places, but not an isolated one. From Cleveland's long-struggling inner suburbs, to the immigrant portals south of Seattle, to aging communities surrounding Chicago, or the traditionally affluent Maryland suburbs of the nation's capital—almost every major metropolitan area in the country has experienced rising

East Contra Costa County, California: An Antioch home converted to rental after the housing market crisis in the late 2000s. (Alex Schafran)

poverty beyond its urban core. Despite the fact that "poverty in America" still conjures images of inner-city slums, the suburbanization of poverty has redrawn the contemporary American landscape. After decades of growth and change in suburbs, coupled with long-term economic restructuring and punctuated by the deepest U.S. economic downturn in seventy years, today more Americans live below the poverty line in suburbs than in the nation's big cities.

Changing populations and shifting economics characterize the experience of suburban communities in East County. These places, which Alex Schafran dubs "Cities of Carquinez" after the nearby Carquinez Strait, were established in the mid- to late nineteenth century.[1] Refineries, factories, mills, working ports, and train and ferry depots dotted the small cities of Pittsburg and Antioch, and unincorporated Bay Point, a century ago. Victorian and Craftsman homes still line the older streets in the portions of these communities near the coastline. Further inland, boomtowns like Brentwood and Oakley retain visible vestiges of their recent agricultural past, when they were western outposts of California's Central Valley rather than eastern suburbs of the Bay Area.

As the Bay Area economy grew and changed in the late twentieth century, however, these East County cities began to shed their farming and industrial character, and exploded in population and new single-family suburban development. The boom was especially rapid in the early to mid-2000s, as a run-up in real estate values in closer-in Bay Area communities made many of these cities an "escape valve" for "drive 'til you qualify" middle-class families seeking affordable homeownership. While their economic heritage meant that these cities had long been home to diverse working-class populations, they also experienced a visible influx of new black and Hispanic residents during this period, most of whom commuted long distances back into the region's core each day for work.

Even amid the relative boom of the early to mid-2000s, broader economic shifts saw the typical household's income in these communities stagnate or fall and the poor population grow, as more residents made their living in quickly growing but lower-wage industries like construction, retail, and hospitality. When the housing market crashed in 2006, however, the economic bottom fell out of East County. Construction workers lost jobs. Families lost wage earners and found themselves slipping down the economic ladder. The subregion became the unofficial foreclosure capital of the Bay Area. At the same time, property investors unable to sell newly built homes recruited low-income renters with government-issued housing vouchers, which gave rise to new community tensions.[2] Local fiscal coffers that relied heavily on property taxes took a beating, even as demand for services skyrocketed.[3] Whereas the poor population had grown more slowly in the earlier part of the decade, the number of people below the poverty line in these relatively small communities rose by nearly 10,000 in the span of just three years—double the increase of the early to mid-2000s.

Not only did these challenges far outstrip the capacity of a strained local public sector, but they also overwhelmed the area's extremely thin nonprofit safety net. Small, local job training organizations could not keep pace with the demand from a burgeoning unemployed population. Foreclosure counselors were in short supply. Most philanthropic dollars in the region remained tethered to historically poor communities in Oakland, San Francisco, or other big cities. Compounding the challenge, the Cities of Carquinez were literally at the "end of the line" in the Bay Area, lacking proximity and transportation options that might help their residents access needed services.

While those eastern Bay Area communities have faced dramatic changes in recent years, their situation mirrors that of an increasing number of suburbs across the United States. This book explores the complicated changes occurring in suburban communities that for several decades defined the middle-class American dream. Why is poverty on the rise there? What are the consequences for those places and their residents? And what, if anything, should society do about it?

Poverty is a relatively new phenomenon in many suburbs, at least at these levels. As such, it upends deeply fixed notions of where poverty occurs and whom it affects. As poverty becomes increasingly regional in its scope and reach, it challenges conventional approaches that the nation has taken when dealing with poverty in place.

Many of those approaches were shaped when President Lyndon B. Johnson declared a national War on Poverty in 1964. At that time, poor Americans were most likely to live in inner-city neighborhoods or sparsely populated rural areas. Fifty years later, public perception still largely casts poverty as an urban or rural phenomenon. Poverty rates do remain higher in cities and rural communities than elsewhere. But for three decades the poor population has grown fastest in suburbs. The especially rapid pace of growth in the 2000s saw suburbs ultimately outstrip other types of communities so that they now account for the largest poor population in the country. More types of people and places are being touched by economic hardship than in the past, including those that may have once seemed immune to such challenges.

The changing map of American poverty matters because place matters.[4] It starts with the metropolitan areas, the regional economies that cut across city and suburban lines and drive the national economy. Place intersects with core policy issues central to the long-term health and stability of metropolitan areas and to the economic success of individuals and families—things like housing, transportation, economic and workforce development, and the provision of education, health, and other basic services. Where people live influences the kinds of educational and economic opportunities and the range of public services available to them, as well as what barriers to accessing those opportunities may exist. The country's deep history of localism means that, within the same metropolitan area, a resident of one community will not necessarily have the same access to good jobs and quality schools, or even basic health and safety services, as a person in another community, whether across the region or right next door.

Poverty's Historic Homes

For decades, experts have framed the debate around the intersection of poverty and place largely in an urban or rural context—for instance, the negative effects of living in an inner-city ghetto or barrio, or the challenges of rural isolation. Poverty rates in these types of communities remain much higher than for the nation as a whole, and for decades these areas have been home to significant portions of the nation's poor, giving rise to an extensive literature that documents the trends and impacts of deep and entrenched poverty in both urban and rural America.

The problems of inner cities received wide attention beginning in the 1960s. In *Tally's Corner*, ethnographer Elliot Liebow documented the lives of the urban poor in the Shaw neighborhood of Washington, D.C. Daniel Patrick Moynihan, a former assistant secretary of labor, issued a controversial report on black poverty arguing that "ghetto culture" and the decline of the nuclear family led to economic hardship.[5] Ken Auletta, Nicholas Lemann, and others followed with portraits of urban "underclass" communities in the 1980s suffering from violent crime, out-of-wedlock childbearing, and eventually the crack cocaine epidemic.[6] Much of this work focused on how the behaviors of poor residents contributed to the deep challenges facing their neighborhoods.

In the 1980s and 1990s, scholar William Julius Wilson posited that structural factors—including the decline of manufacturing jobs for lower-skilled city workers—led to a rise in joblessness that increased poverty and ultimately affected cultural norms and behaviors in declining urban neighborhoods.[7] He also argued that growing concentrations of poverty in predominantly minority, inner-city areas undermined community institutions and networks formerly maintained by middle-class and working-class families, and removed positive role models for children, helping to perpetuate the cycle of poverty.[8] Douglas Massey and Nancy Denton explored how the legacy of racial segregation shaped contemporary urban poverty in the early 1990s.[9]

Paul Jargowsky and others went on to document trends in concentrated poverty across the country, finding the largest concentrations of the poor in inner-city neighborhoods with much higher shares of minorities, single mothers, high school dropouts, and working-age men outside the labor force than in areas with less poverty.[10] Others, including George Galster, examined the thresholds at which concentrations of poverty led to appreciable negative effects on residents, neighborhoods, and the larger region that housed them, including poorer health and educational outcomes, increased crime, and falling property values.[11]

In a parallel vein over this same time period, rural poverty experts explored the persistence and depth of poverty in the nation's wide-ranging and far-flung rural communities. These explorations focused on structural factors in the community as well as individual characteristics of the poor, including the decline of traditional industries, out-migration, and low educational levels.[12] Janet Fitchen chronicled the persistence of generational poverty in rural households in upstate New York, finding that contemporary families were unable to adapt to economic shifts toward modern agriculture.[13] Looking at Appalachia and the Mississippi Delta, Cynthia Duncan found that places with greater evidence of multigenerational poverty were also home to social structures that isolated people with lower incomes from better-off residents, inhibiting social mobility.[14] Regardless of the mechanisms at play, poverty in rural communities and across generations has proven a seemingly intractable, and in fact growing, issue. Children in rural areas today are more likely than a generation ago to live in communities plagued by persistently high poverty over decades.[15]

The Dawn of the Modern Suburb

In contrast, suburbs have traditionally inhabited a very different popular narrative in American culture, one in which poverty generally does not feature (except perhaps to the extent that the rise of the suburbs signaled—and even contributed to—urban decline). In many ways, suburbs have been central to the particular brand of the American dream that developed rapidly after World War II. Moving to suburbia signaled a step up—a house with a yard, a car to drive to work, good schools, and safe streets. As Bernadette Hanlon and her colleagues noted:

> The very pursuit of happiness in post-war history was synonymous with the suburbs. A move to the suburbs symbolized many things in the American context. It was a move of social and economic mobility: a path that led away from the nation's ailing central cities and to the emergent suburban frontier. The American Dream was realized in the nation's nascent suburbs.[16]

Perhaps most emblematic of the fast-growing suburban communities that multiplied in the postwar era were the developments built by Abraham Levitt and his sons William and Alfred. In the Levittowns built on Long Island, and outside Philadelphia (in Bucks County, Pennsylvania, and Willingboro, New Jersey), Levitt and Sons honed their approach to suburban development, using a standardized housing design, preassembled parts, and vertical integration of suppliers to speed production. Regarding these cookie-cutter Cape Cods with a living room, a bathroom, two bedrooms, a kitchen, and a yard, Kenneth Jackson observed, "This early Levitt house was as basic to post World War II suburban development as the Model T had been to the automobile. In each case, the actual design features were less important than the fact that they were mass-produced and thus priced within reach of the middle class."[17] Jackson also noted that while Levitt did not invent many of the techniques he employed, the wide publicity of his developments served to popularize his approach. Large builders in metropolitan areas throughout the country—including developers in Boston, Chicago, Cleveland, Denver, Houston, Los Angeles, Phoenix, San Francisco, and Washington—adopted similar methods.[18]

The rapid build-out of the suburbs in that period reflected both the pull of and the push toward suburbia. William Lucy and David Phillips observed that "individual preferences provided the motivation, and development institutions and policies . . . provided the means" that drove suburban growth, often led by affluent households.[19] Aging and declining urban infrastructure, pollution, poor schools, and perceptions of rising crime in central cities, coupled with the promise of new, single-family homes, clean air, and green spaces, made the burgeoning suburbs all the more desirable.[20] The draw of the suburbs reached across class lines, yet affluent households—especially those headed by middle- and upper-class whites—were able to act on those preferences more readily, particularly when aided by policies and institutions that paved the way (sometimes literally) for the move to the suburbs.

The "means" Lucy and Phillips refer to came from an array of programs and policies that enabled and encouraged large-scale suburbanization. According to Kevin Kruse and Thomas Sugrue:

> Public policies, including federal housing and economic development subsidies, state and local land-use policies and environmental regulations, locally administered services and taxation policies, and locally controlled schools, all inexorably shaped the process of suburbanization in the postwar period. The division of metropolitan areas by race and class, a division that was reified and reinforced through the drawing of hard municipal boundaries, created a distinct form of spatialized inequality in the modern United States.[21]

At the federal level, a range of programs and policies contributed to rapid suburbanization in this period, whether by encouraging and easing the way to homeownership or heavily subsidizing the roads and sewers needed to support "greenfield" development at the urban fringe.[22] For prospective home buyers, insured mortgages through the Federal Housing Administration (FHA) and the GI Bill's Veterans Affairs (VA) mortgage program freed up the flow of private capital for home loans. Further subsidies for homeowners came in the form of federal tax breaks, like the home mortgage interest deduction. The Federal-Aid Highway Act of 1956, which covered 90 percent of the cost of highway construction, set in motion the rapid development of the interstate highway system that not only connected major regions across the country but enabled suburban development to extend deeper into the countryside with the promise of easier commutes for would-be suburbanites.[23] In that same year, Congress enacted legislation to subsidize more than half the cost of new sewer treatment facilities, further facilitating the development of the infrastructure needed to support suburban growth.[24]

As these federal investments drove the widespread suburbanization of a predominantly white middle class, other people and places faced disinvestment. For instance, the tax code provided an open-ended subsidy for homeowners but allowed no parallel housing benefit for renters.[25] For homeowners, the most favorable home loans went to new construction, while loans for improvements or rehabilitation were smaller and given for shorter durations. All of these factors favored suburban development over central cities. Moreover, federal loan insurance programs essentially codified the private market's practice of redlining, curtailing lending to inner cities and minorities. From 1945 to 1959, approximately 90 percent of all FHA and VA mortgages were for suburban homes, yet fewer than 2 percent went to African Americans.[26] At the same time, federal investments in roads enabled the rise of the auto-dependent suburbs rather than encouraging denser development around mass transit.[27] Andres Duany and his colleagues observed that the nation's suburban expansion lacked "incentives to integrate different housing types or incomes among the new construction. In a sense our government did half its job: it provided the means to escape the city—highways and cheap home loans—while neglecting to allocate those means fairly."[28]

Beyond the federal actions (or inaction) that helped spur suburban development, state and local policies also created critical barriers to entry that increased inequality across metropolitan communities. Policy decisions at the state and local level around public housing, transportation, taxation, the provision of services, annexation, land use, and zoning made it possible for growing suburbs to exclude low-income and minority residents, widening the gap between lower-income cities and their more affluent suburban neighbors.[29] Charles Tilly described this as "opportunity hoarding," where suburban municipalities draw boundaries and incorporate in a way that perpetuates inequality through the differing levels of services they provide—and taxes they charge—to residents.[30] Jonathan Rothwell and Douglas Massey found a strong relationship between density zoning in the suburbs and increased income segregation, suggesting that restrictive zoning practices exacerbate income and racial inequality within regions.[31]

That suburban narrative is the one most Americans are familiar with: the suburbs as middle- and upper-class bastions, built as predominantly white, well-off residents moved away from cities, leaving minority and lower-income populations to deal with growing urban problems and a shrinking tax base. These dynamics were indeed at play, but the history of suburban America remains more complex.

The Rise of Suburban Poverty

Suburbs have never been as monolithic as historical stereotypes would suggest. Suburbanization in the prewar period included residents of all classes. Low-income residents have long been a part of suburban development, from those who were among the first to suburbanize more than a century ago in pursuit of cheaper land at the outskirts of urban areas, to members of emerging immigrant enclaves, to residents of blue-collar communities who went to work providing services in more affluent neighboring suburbs.[32] While postwar policies created additional and significant barriers to entry for low-income residents in many growing suburbs, over time even the new postwar suburbs eventually saw their housing stock age, and some experienced broader economic decline as industries waned or moved out.

In the 1990s, researchers began to chronicle the diversity that exists across American suburbs, paying particular attention to older, declining suburbs.[33] Lucy and Phillips found suburban decline to be most prevalent in post–World War II car-dependent suburbs with deteriorating modest single-family houses. These places also tended to have public and private institutions that lacked a sufficient commitment to reinvestment in private homes and public infrastructure.[34] Similarly, Myron Orfield and Robert Puentes identified inner-ring "first" suburbs as places built early in or toward the middle of the twentieth century. While many of these communities continue to be healthy and stable, over time others became home to aging infrastructure and inadequate housing stock, as well as deteriorating schools and commercial corridors.[35] Many of the most distressed first suburbs in midwestern and northeastern metropolitan areas—manufacturing-based, older industrial areas struggling with structural shifts and economic decline. These suburbs had lost population or had grown slowly, and were home not only to older housing stock but also to older and shrinking households.[36] Orfield estimated that as many as 40 percent of residents in the nation's largest metropolitan regions lived in "at-risk" older communities, typified by meager local resources, struggling commercial districts, and slow or no population growth.[37]

These findings laid an important foundation for understanding the transitions and challenges facing suburban communities throughout the country. However, the magnitude and pace of growth in suburban poverty after 2000 far outstripped these earlier indications of inner-ring suburban economic decline. The first decade of the twenty-first century saw two recessions coupled with weak and jobless recoveries, as well as continued structural shifts in the economy that contributed to a shrinking middle class and falling income for the typical household. The economic tumult of the 2000s not only helped propel the size of America's poor population to record levels but also contributed to its broadening geographic reach. Rising poverty touched all kinds of communities around the country, moving well beyond the declining and at-risk suburbs chronicled in earlier research and reframing the challenges of poverty as regional issues.

Despite these trends, the public policy framework for addressing poverty in place in the United States remains largely urban-oriented and ill-equipped to address the geographic scale of today's need. That need, of course, has not left urban areas but has grown well beyond their borders. Moreover, the problems of regionalizing poverty have been exacerbated by a weak economy and increasingly limited resources for nonprofits, philanthropies, and government at all levels.

At the same time, the unprecedented growth of unemployment and poverty in the suburbs during the 2000s reflects structural shifts in the economy that pose serious challenges for antipoverty policy. By 2010, one in three Americans was poor or near poor, meaning that 104 million people lived below twice the federal poverty line—23 million more than in 2000 (an increase almost the size of the population of Texas). With the U.S. population projected to grow to 400 million by 2050, even a return to prerecession trends would mean another 19 million people in or near poverty. Without a change in course, poverty is likely to reach deeper into the nation's metropolitan regions, even as it continues to concentrate in distressed inner-city and suburban locales. Current systems for addressing poverty cannot simply be refined; they must be reformed and remade to respond to the realities of contemporary metropolitan America.

As the nation struggles to find its footing in the emerging economic recovery, it has the opportunity (and the imperative) to avoid repeating the mistakes of the last boom-and-bust cycle that left so many Americans behind in the 2000s, eroding middle-wage jobs and fueling rising inequality. Making progress against poverty means crafting policies and programs that connect residents to the kinds of educational, job, and housing opportunities that can help them better their economic situations. In turn, metropolitan areas benefit in the long run when they forge those kinds of connections and help build a diverse, educated, and skilled workforce.

To ensure that the next economy this country builds is an opportunity-rich economy, a reformed and remade antipoverty framework must be flexible and built to the scale of the challenge. Suburbs offer, in a way, a "clean slate" upon which to design a new and more effective approach to promoting opportunity. Implementing a place-based policy agenda and infrastructure built to work in the suburbs does not mean turning away from the significant need that persists in urban and rural America. Rather, such a framework has the potential to better alleviate poverty and increase access to opportunity throughout the country, with improvements in flexibility and efficiency accruing not just to the suburbs, but to the urban and rural poor as well.

This book provides the foundation for a twenty-first-century metropolitan opportunity agenda. Much of the research presented here originated with the Brookings Metropolitan Opportunity Series, a research series funded by the Ford Foundation and the Annie E. Casey Foundation that since 2009 has documented city and suburban poverty trends and analyzed the drivers and implications of the shifting geography of poverty and opportunity. A number of Brookings researchers and partners have contributed publications to the series over the years, all of which are available on the Brookings website and offer detailed findings on the trends, causes, and challenges related to the suburbanization of poverty. This book updates and extends that research, most notably by describing the experiences of a range of suburban areas across the country that we visited during 2011 and 2012, interviewing local leaders and practitioners about the causes and consequences of growing poverty in their communities.

The following three chapters map the diverse ways in which the growth of suburban poverty has occurred across the nation's largest metropolitan regions and examines the implications for families and communities:

—Chapter 2 documents shifts in poverty within and across the cities and suburbs in the nation's largest metropolitan areas and across different racial and ethnic groups. It also examines the similarities and differences among poor residents in cities and suburbs, across an array of demographic and economic characteristics.

—Chapter 3 turns to drivers of the suburbanization of poverty in the 2000s. How did economic factors, employment location, population and immigration trends, and housing help shape suburban poverty's rise? We draw on a combination of quantitative research and qualitative examples from site visits in diverse metropolitan areas to answer these questions.

—Chapter 4 details the impact of growing suburban poverty—from challenges related to accessing transportation and employment to the increased strain on a patchy and thin safety net, to the experience of schools—on different regions and kinds of places. We group the diverse array of suburbs experiencing growing poverty into community types in ways that could guide policy responses.

The final three chapters of the book turn to the policy outlook in the context of regionalizing poverty:

—Chapter 5 details the limits of existing policy, as well as the challenges and barriers that complicate the effective extension of the current policy framework into suburbia.

—Chapter 6 presents lessons learned from a network of leaders operating in regions throughout the country. These innovators have found ways to work within (and often around) the current framework, overcoming shortcomings in the system to deliver services and policy interventions more effectively. These lessons help lay the foundation for a new direction in policy and practice.

—Chapter 7, the final chapter, outlines a next-generation agenda for enhancing opportunity within metropolitan America. It offers a series of short- and long-term recommendations for federal, state, and local policymakers, as well as business, philanthropic, and nonprofit leaders grappling with the new realities of suburban poverty.

A final introductory note: In *Confronting Suburban Poverty*, we do not take the view that poverty in the suburbs is necessarily *better* or *worse* for families or for society than in other locales. Instead, we aim to understand how it is *different* in its origins, its consequences, and its implications for policy. As this book shows, many low-income families in suburbs—whether recent arrivals or long-time residents—are living in safer neighborhoods with access to higher-quality schools than their counterparts in poor inner-city neighborhoods. But as many low-income residents of Oakland and Richmond, California, discovered when they moved to the Cities of Carquinez (profiled at the beginning of this chapter), suburban life can also mean greater isolation from transportation, social services, employment, and community support.

We believe that the goal of public policy must be to provide all families with access to communities, whether in cities or suburbs, that offer a high quality of life and solid platform for upward mobility over time. Understanding the new reality of poverty in metropolitan America is a critical step toward realizing that goal.

CHAPTER 2

Suburban Poverty, by the Numbers

Lakewood, Ohio, hugs the city of Cleveland's northwest border. It is an architecturally diverse community. Some of its 50,000-plus residents live in Tudor homes in beautiful neighborhoods along Lake Erie. Others live in high-rise apartment buildings in the city's nearby Gold Coast section. Still others live in smaller bungalows and multifamily duplexes that line Lakewood's dense street grid. It is a quintessential "streetcar" suburb that blends the residential and the commercial. As a social, creative, and artistic hub, it continues to be a desirable location for many of the region's residents.

Yet increasingly, Lakewood is an economically diverse community. By 2008–10, 16 percent of its residents lived below the poverty line, up from 9 percent in 2000. Between 1998–99 and 2009–10, the share of Lakewood High students receiving free and reduced-price lunches increased dramatically, from 9 to 46 percent. Lakewood's low-income

Lakewood, Ohio: Duplexes and two-story apartment buildings, largely rental units, west of downtown. (Chris Garr)

Box 2-1. A Note on Terms

Decades of research on the geography of American poverty has brought to bear different benchmarks of economic hardship and has drawn the boundaries of metropolitan, urban, and suburban communities in different ways. In the analysis presented here, we use the following definitions:

Poverty

For comparisons over time and across places, we use the official U.S. federal poverty thresholds (for example, $22,314 for a family of four in 2010) as the primary measure of the poor population.[a] This measure is not without its shortcomings, which have been well documented.[b] Yet the federal thresholds provide a consistent (and perhaps conservative) benchmark by which to measure trends in income poverty over time and across places. U.S. Census Bureau data based on this definition are available down to the neighborhood level, going back several decades.

Data

This analysis uses poverty and demographic data from the U.S. Census Bureau's decennial census and American Community Survey (ACS). The ACS has replaced the decennial long-form survey, which was the source of income and poverty estimates through Census 2000. Differences between the surveys should be noted. For instance, the 2000 decennial census was administered at one point in time (April) and asked about income in the preceding calendar year, whereas the ACS is administered every month and asks about income "in the last 12 months." Monthly ACS results are combined and adjusted for inflation to create single-year estimates. In addition, the ACS surveys a much smaller sample than the long-form census does (for example, 3 million households per year versus roughly 19 million in 2000).

Where possible, in this analysis we use single-year ACS estimates, which are available for geographies with populations of 65,000 or more. Because of issues with sample size, we sometimes use three-year estimates (available for geographies with populations of at least 20,000) or five-year estimates to get to the geographic level of detail of a smaller suburban jurisdiction or neighborhood. We note the use of multiyear estimates by referencing the years represented by the data (for example, 2008–10 or 2006–10). Also, in recognition of sample-size issues, we test for statistical significance when making comparisons with these data. Throughout the analysis, any changes or differences noted are statistically significant at the 90 percent confidence level.

Owing to data availability, and for ease and completeness of analysis, most of our comparisons occur across decades (for example, 1990 to 2000, 2000 to 2010), rather than across business cycles (for example, 1991 to 2000, 2001 to 2007). Thus, trends reflect cyclical as well as structural changes in the incidence and distribution of poverty.

Geography

We apply the same geographic definitions to each year of data analyzed to preserve comparability over time. We start with the 366 metropolitan statistical areas designated by the U.S. Office of Management and Budget in 2010.[c] *Large metropolitan areas* include the 100 most populous metropolitan areas in that year. The remaining metropolitan areas fall into the *small metropolitan area* category. Any county outside of a metropolitan statistical area is considered to be *nonmetropolitan* (also referred to as *rural*).

Within the 100 largest metropolitan areas, we identify primary cities and suburbs. *Primary cities* (also referred to as *cities*) are those that appear first in the official metropolitan statistical area name and any other cities in the official name that have populations of at least 100,000.[d] *Suburbs* make up the remainder of the metropolitan areas outside of primary cities.

Defining Suburban America

No one definition of "suburb" exists. Some researchers have defined suburbs as anything outside the first-named city in a metropolitan area. In contrast, the U.S. Census Bureau often refers to suburbs as areas outside of census-identified "principal cities," which often exceed the number of cities in the official metropolitan area name. (For example, in the Los Angeles–Long Beach–Santa Ana, California, Metropolitan Statistical Area, the Census Bureau identifies twenty-five principal cities, meaning that places such as Arcadia, Fountain Valley, and Tustin count alongside Los Angeles as cities rather than suburbs.)

The definition we adopt strikes a balance between these two approaches, though it is admittedly imperfect in that it combines a wide array of communities—from older urban places that look and feel like cities (for example, White Plains, New York; Dearborn, Michigan; Frederick, Maryland) to newer lower-density places (for example, Maricopa, Arizona; Conroe, Texas; Castle Rock, Colorado)—under the umbrella term "suburb." In chapter 4 we introduce a more nuanced typology to acknowledge and address the diversity that exists in suburbia, moving below the net metropolitan-area suburban totals to disaggregate counties and incorporated places. Nevertheless, the "suburban" aggregate used throughout much of this analysis represents a compromise that distinguishes within each metropolitan area between large, broadly recognized jurisdictions and smaller places that are more likely to lack the scale and capacity necessary to address some of the challenges of rising poverty.

a. Other common measures of "low income" include 80 percent of area median income (AMI)—often used by the U.S. Department of Housing and Urban Development—and twice the federal poverty line. See, for example, the Working Poor Families Project, "Still Working Hard, Still Falling Short: New Findings on the Challenges Confronting America's Working Families" (Washington, 2008), www.workingpoorfamilies.org/about/. We use these measures at selected points in the analysis, as noted, but rely primarily on the official poverty measure for consistency and comparability across places and over time.

b. For detailed discussion of the federal poverty measure, see, for example, National Academy of Sciences (NAS), *Measuring Poverty: A New Approach* (Washington: National Academy Press, 1995). The Census Bureau began releasing the Supplemental Poverty Measure in 2011 that takes into account recommendations from the 1995 NAS study, including adjusting for regional differences in cost of living and factoring in after-tax income and cash and in-kind benefits. However, because the estimates are based on data from the Current Population Survey, the sample size is not sufficient to report estimates for substate geographies. In addition, historical data by which to evaluate trends over time are not available.

c. The 2010 definitions are used in the analyses throughout chapter 2. In later chapters that refer to findings from earlier papers in the Metropolitan Opportunity Series, slight differences in the list of 100 metropolitan areas and primary cities used may exist, as noted in the methods sections of those briefs.

d. American Community Survey (ACS) single-year estimates—which replaced the decennial census long form—are available only for places with a population of 65,000 or more. Five metropolitan areas in 2010 had primary cities with populations below that threshold: those surrounding Greenville, South Carolina; Harrisburg and Lancaster, Pennsylvania; North Port, Florida; and Poughkeepsie, New York. When using the single-year estimates, those metropolitan areas are grouped in the small metropolitan area category and not included in the city and suburban analyses.

population includes workers and the long-term unemployed; whites, African Americans, immigrants, and refugees; and children, working-age adults, and seniors.

This suburban community provides a snapshot of the challenges facing cities and towns throughout the greater Cleveland area today. The loss of manufacturing jobs in the 2000s, punctuated by an even more rapid decline during the Great Recession, exacted a terrible toll on the regional economy. Workers lost employment and income, and families lost homes to foreclosure. Lakewood's unemployment rate, which had hovered below 3 percent as recently as 2001, exceeded 8 percent in 2010.

Lakewood also faces specific challenges that arise from its history, location, and size. Well over half of its housing stock was built in the early twentieth century—much of it for manufacturing workers, including those from the local Union Carbide plant—and has weathered decades of disinvestment. Because the community shares a border with the city of Cleveland, Lakewood is also the first stop for many low-income individuals and families, some with significant barriers to work, who are looking for better schools or housing options or are seeking escape from unsafe or undesirable neighborhoods in Cleveland. However, although the community has a history of collaborative and progressive local leadership, Lakewood is not a large enough municipality on its own to carry out needed housing-code enforcement or deliver social services at scale. Overstretched local social service providers attract modest but limited philanthropic support, given the long shadow of Lakewood's needy next-door neighbor.

Lakewood's history and pattern of development are different from that of the eastern Bay Area suburbs described at the start of chapter 1. Yet both are at the forefront of the seminal trend explored in detail in this chapter: a rapid suburbanization of poverty that gripped old and new places alike.

The Rise of Suburban Poverty: The Big Picture

This inquiry into the suburbanization of poverty focuses on the nation's 100 most populous metropolitan areas. In 2010, these metropolitan regions—which correspond roughly to those areas with populations of at least 500,000—were home to nearly two-thirds (65 percent) of the nation's population, from the megametropolis of greater New York (population 19 million) to the Central Valley region of Modesto, California (population 514,000). In contrast to many smaller metropolitan areas, these 100 regions capture what most Americans would regard as the nation's important and recognizable urban centers and their suburbs. These regions' share of the nation's population is little changed from 1970, when the footprint of today's 100 largest metropolitan areas contained 63 percent of the country's residents.

The geography of the nation's poor, however, changed markedly over the ensuing forty years, shifting decidedly away from smaller communities and toward these large metropolitan areas. In 1970, just over half of the country's poor population lived in the counties that make up these metropolitan areas today. Four decades later, that share had risen to 61 percent—nearly catching up to those areas' share of the overall U.S. population.

As the balance of the nation's poor population shifted away from rural communities and toward the country's largest economic centers, the location of the poor within metropolitan America began to change as well (see figure 2-1). In 1970, 30 percent of the nation's poor lived outside of any metropolitan area. Another 27 percent resided in the major cities that anchor the nation's largest metropolitan regions. Fewer than 24 percent were located in the suburbs of these metropolitan areas, and another 20 percent lived in what are today's smaller metropolitan hubs—regions such as Atlantic City, New Jersey; Bloomington, Indiana; and Redding, California. By 1980, the share of the poor housed in rural communities had already slipped below that in both big cities and suburbs. Between 1980 and 2000, just over 30 percent of the nation's poor population lived in cities.

During this period, small shifts began to emerge in the location of poverty that heralded larger transformations in the years to follow. Poor populations continued to increase in both cities and suburbs during the 1980s and 1990s, but the rate of growth in the suburban poor population began to outpace that of cities for the first time (Figure 2-2). During the 1990s, the number of poor individuals in suburbs grew at more than twice that in cities—19 percent compared with 8 percent.

This trend accelerated strikingly in the 2000s. From 2000 to 2010, the nation's poor population grew from 33.9 million to a record 46.2 million. As this occurred, the number of poor individuals living in the suburbs of the nation's largest metropolitan areas rose by more than half (53 percent), or 5.3 million (see figure 2-3). This was more than twice the rate of increase in cities, where the poor population grew by 23 percent, or 2.4 million.

Figure 2-1. Distribution of the U.S. Poor Population by Community Type, 1970 to 2000

Percent

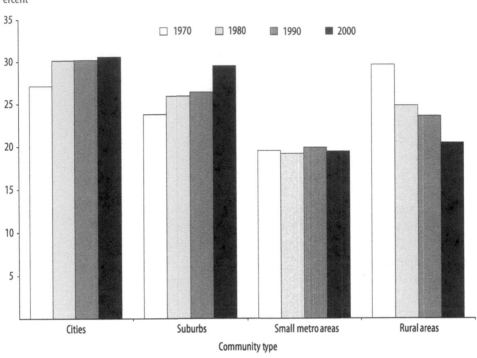

Source: Brookings Institution analysis of decennial census data.

With this dramatic expansion in suburban poverty during the 2000s, metropolitan America crossed an economic Rubicon: for the first time, more of its poor lived in suburbs than in cities. As revealed by the first complete year of ACS data, this shift had already occurred by the middle of the decade, and the increase continued steadily through the rest of the 2000s. By 2010, 15.3 million poor individuals—55 percent of the metropolitan poor population—lived in suburbs, almost 2.6 million more than in cities (12.8 million). Nationally, by the end of the 2000s one in three poor Americans lived in the suburbs, making them home to the largest and fastest-growing poor population in the country.

Economic hardship, of course, does not end at the federal poverty line. A number of researchers have argued that setting the definition of "low income" at twice the federal poverty line is a more realistic reflection of the income necessary for a family to afford essentials, including food, housing, transportation, and health care.[1] The "near-poor," those

Figure 2-2. Growth Rates in City and Suburban Poor Populations, 1970 to 2010

Time period

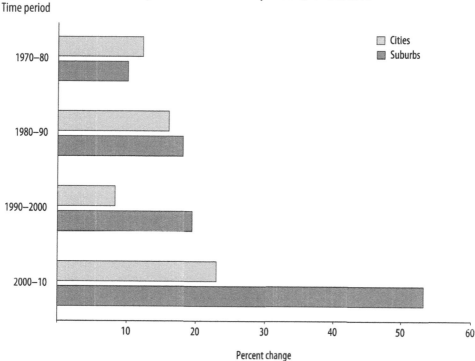

Percent change

Source: Brookings Institution analysis of decennial census and ACS data.

with incomes between 100 and 200 percent of the poverty line, are even more suburbanized than those below the poverty line (see figure 2-4). By 2010, 63 percent of near-poor metropolitan residents—22 million people—lived in suburbs, up from 59 percent in 2000 and well above the 55 percent of poor metropolitan-area residents in suburbs. Altogether, more than one in four suburban residents were poor or near-poor in 2010, which suggests that the scope of economic hardship in suburbia is even larger than that captured by official poverty numbers.

However, even with these significant transitions in the landscape of metropolitan poverty, urban poverty did not diminish. Residents of cities were still more likely to be poor than their suburban neighbors (see figure 2-5). In 2010, just over one in five urban residents lived in poverty (21 percent), compared with roughly one in nine people living in suburbs (11 percent). In fact, suburbs continued to exhibit a lower poverty rate than cities, small metropolitan areas, and nonmetropolitan

Figure 2-3. Number of Poor Residents in Cities and Suburbs, 1970 to 2010
Millions

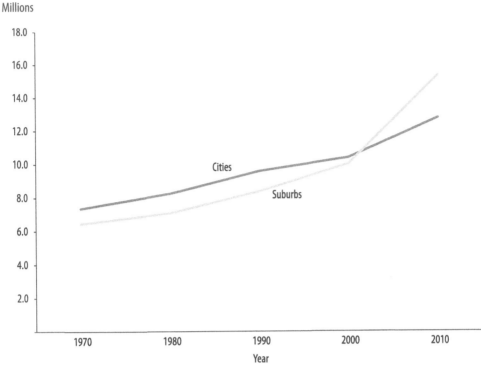

Source: Brookings Institution analysis of decennial census and ACS data.

areas. This was the case even after the suburban poverty rate rose by nearly 3 percentage points in the 2000s, which was on par with the increase in cities and in the nation as a whole.

The size and persistence of the disparity between city and suburban poverty rates illuminate two important trends. First, the long-running challenges of urban poverty in the nation's largest metropolitan areas remained—and in fact worsened—even as economic hardship reached deeper into the surrounding region. Poverty did not trade one location for the other but instead affected both cities and suburbs as it grew. Second, given the much larger size of suburbia—its population is more than double that of cities—"keeping pace" on the poverty rate means that the suburban poor population expanded by a much greater margin than the poor population in cities.

Figure 2-4. Distribution of the Near-Poor Population in the Nation's Largest Metropolitan Areas, 2000 and 2010

Year

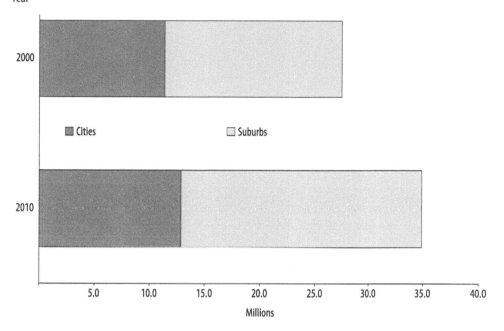

Source: Brookings Institution analysis of decennial census and ACS data.

A Regional Perspective on Suburban Poverty

Most places across the country have experienced this rise in suburban poverty, yet marked regional differences remain in its origins, trajectory, and contemporary magnitude. These differences owe in part to the age and history of metropolitan areas. Postwar suburbs in older industrial areas of the Midwest and Northeast were particularly characterized by the kinds of exclusionary development practices explored in chapter 1, including restrictive zoning, redlining, and limits on annexation, that left many central cities hemmed in and unable to absorb prosperous neighboring suburbs. In these areas, low-income and minority populations remain much less suburbanized than other groups, with poor residents lagging behind the total population by roughly 20 percentage points in 2010 (see figure 2-6). By contrast, newer metropolitan areas in the West and South, many of which feature large suburban cities and

Figure 2-5. Poverty Rate by Community Type, 2000 and 2010

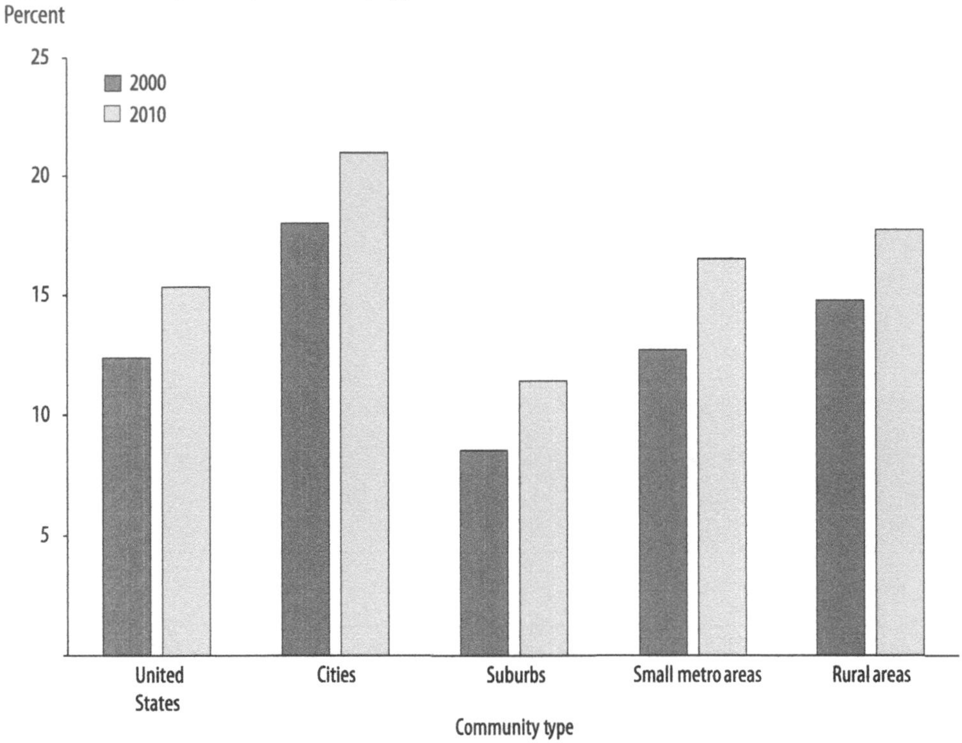

Percent

Source: Brookings Institution analysis of decennial census and ACS data.

agricultural areas, exhibit narrower disparities—closer to 10 percentage points—between the suburbanization of the poor and the nonpoor.

Seattle provides one example of the dominant pattern in the West. Even before 2000, its suburbs had more poor residents—61 percent of the metropolitan total—than the cities of Seattle, Tacoma, and Bellevue combined. Over the course of the subsequent decade, greater Seattle's suburban poor population grew by three-quarters (74 percent), compared with a rise of 26 percent in cities. By 2010, more than two-thirds (68 percent) of the metropolitan area's poor lived in suburbs, which is almost on par with their share of the total population (73 percent).

In the South, Atlanta's experience has been similar to Seattle's, though more dramatic. Atlanta's metropolitan area extends over a vast stretch of territory, covering twenty-eight counties and more than 8,400 square miles (almost 2,500 square miles more than metropolitan Seattle). In 2000, 76 percent of the region's poor resided in Atlanta's suburbs. In the

Figure 2-6. Share of Metropolitan-Area Population in Suburbs by Poverty Status and Region, 2010

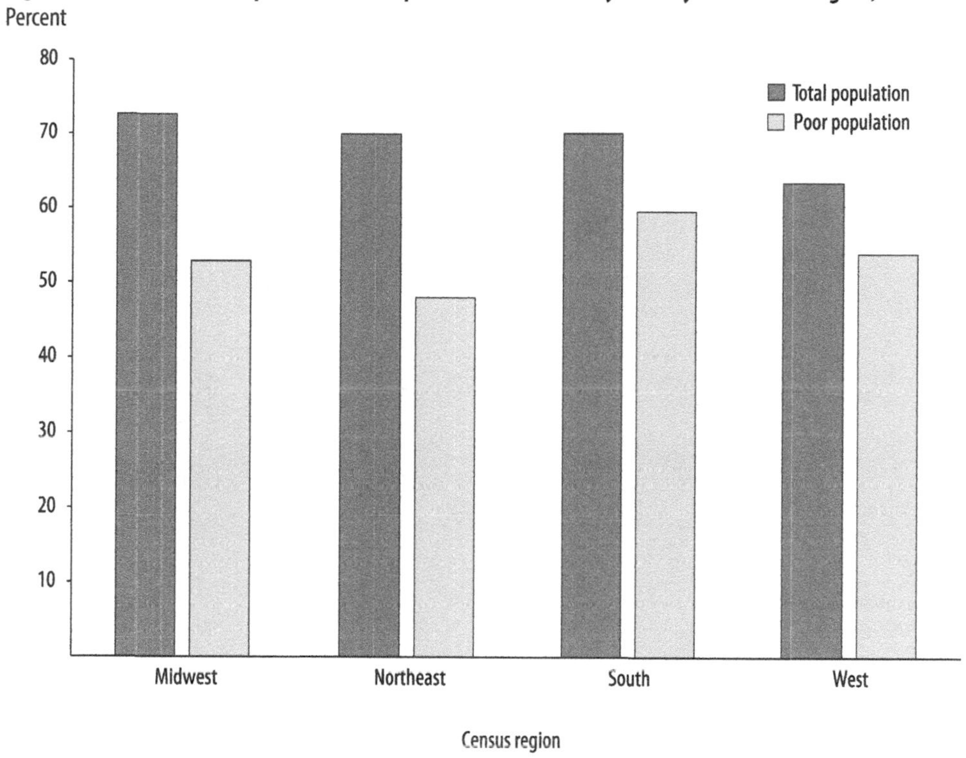

Percent

Census region

Source: Brookings Institution analysis of ACS data.

ten years that followed, the number of suburban poor more than doubled while the city of Atlanta's poor population remained statistically unchanged. The precipitous increase in Atlanta's suburban poverty pushed the region's share of poor living in suburbs up to 87 percent, not far from the proportion of its total population living in suburbia (92 percent).

Even in the Midwest and Northeast, where historical economic divisions between cities and suburbs have been starker and longer running, the 2000s marked a sea change. In metropolitan Chicago, more than two-thirds of the region's population lives in the suburbs surrounding the cities of Chicago, Naperville, and Joliet. Yet in 2000, the suburbs were home to only 39 percent of the region's poor. Over the course of the decade, the number of suburban poor grew by 76 percent, compared with an uptick of just 10 percent in the region's urban hubs. As a result, by 2010, for the first time a majority of greater Chicago's poor population (51 percent) lived in suburbs.

Figure 2-7. Percentage Change in the Suburban Poor Population, 2000 to 2010

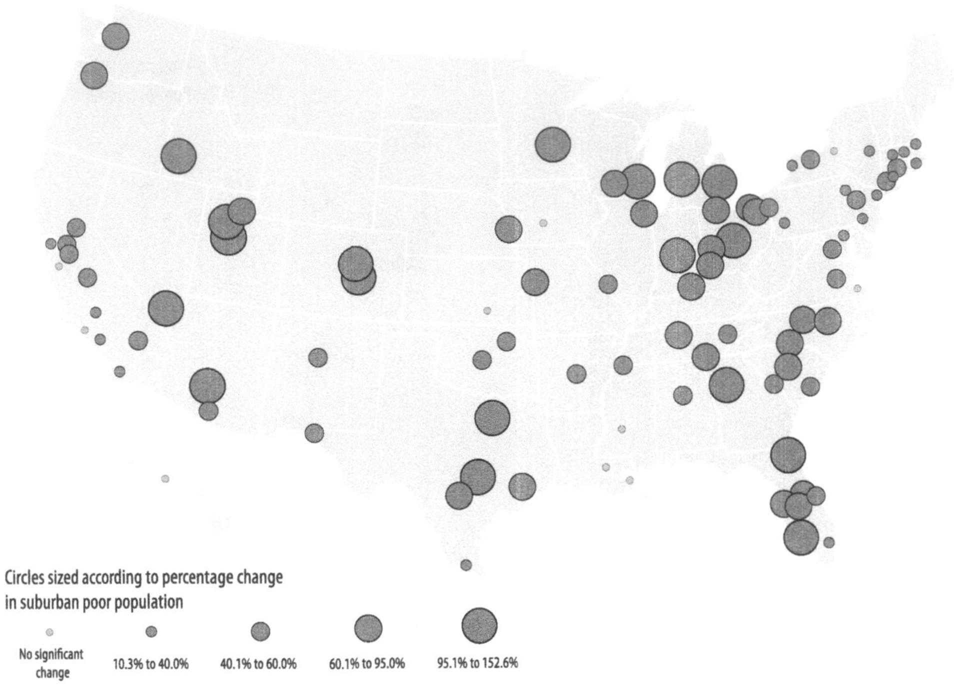

Circles sized according to percentage change
in suburban poor population

No significant change	10.3% to 40.0%	40.1% to 60.0%	60.1% to 95.0%	95.1% to 152.6%

Source: Brookings Institution analysis of decennial census and ACS data.

Metropolitan Chicago was not the only region in the Midwest to pass this tipping point. The experience of Lakewood, described at the start of this chapter, is indicative of a larger regional shift in the balance of metropolitan poverty during the 2000s. The Cleveland region and the Detroit and Minneapolis–St. Paul metropolitan areas each began the decade with roughly 46 percent of their poor populations living in suburbs. All three regions ended the 2000s with a majority of their poor populations located in suburbia.

By 2010, sixty regions scattered throughout the country found the majority of their poor in the suburbs. The next chapter delves into the various factors that helped to drive the spread of poverty in these communities, but figure 2-7 illustrates the diversity of places that experienced growth in their suburban poor populations, and it hints at the range of experiences that accompanied those trends. Growing (Phoenix) or contracting (Detroit), struggling (Las Vegas) or thriving (Houston),

Table 2-1. Metropolitan Areas with the Largest Increases in City and Suburban Poverty Rates, 2000 to 2010

	Suburban poverty			Primary city poverty	
Metropolitan area[a]	Poverty rate 2000–10 (% point change)	Poverty rate 2010 (percent)	Metropolitan area[a]	Poverty rate 2000–10 (% point change)	Poverty rate 2010 (percent)
Cape Coral, Fla.	8.0	18.6	Grand Rapids, Mich.	14.3	30.0
Greensboro-High Point, N.C.	6.7	15.6	Akron, Ohio	11.9	29.4
Colorado Springs, Colo.	6.0	12.4	Dayton, Ohio	11.5	34.5
Atlanta, Ga.	5.9	13.9	Ogden, Utah	11.2	27.7
Grand Rapids, Mich.	5.8	12.1	Detroit-Warren, Mich.	11.2	34.9
Dayton, Ohio	5.8	12.8	Indianapolis, Ind.	9.3	21.1
Detroit-Warren, Mich.	5.8	12.1	Boise City, Idaho	8.9	17.3
Youngstown, Ohio-Pa.	5.8	15.2	Cincinnati, Ohio-Ky.-Ind.	8.7	30.6
Boise City, Idaho	5.6	15.6	Allentown, Penn.-N.J.	8.5	27.0
Salt Lake City, Utah	5.1	11.3	Milwaukee, Wis.	8.2	29.5
Lakeland, Fla.	5.1	17.7	Kansas City, Mo.-Kan.	8.2	25.3
Jacksonville, Fla.	5.1	13.1	Palm Bay, Fla.	8.0	17.5
Tampa-St. Petersburg-Clearwater, Fla.	4.6	14.1	Greensboro-High Point, N.C.	7.9	20.5
Las Vegas, Nev.	4.5	14.7	Toledo, Ohio	7.9	25.8
Columbus, Ohio	4.5	10.5	Rochester, N.Y.	7.9	33.8

Source: Brookings Institution analysis of decennial census and ACS data.

a. Metropolitan area names have been adjusted to reflect Brookings Institution–defined primary cities.

Sun Belt (Tampa) or Rust Belt (St. Louis), few metropolitan areas proved immune to increasing suburban poverty. During the 2000s, the suburban poor population grew by a significant margin in eighty-five of the nation's ninety-five largest metropolitan areas. Fully sixteen of these regions saw their suburban poor population more than double in the span of ten years, including Atlanta; Boise; Cape Coral, Florida; Colorado Springs; Columbus, Ohio; Grand Rapids, Michigan; Jacksonville, Florida; Las Vegas; Phoenix; and Salt Lake City.

Expanding suburban poor populations pushed poverty rates up in nearly as many regions: seventy-five metropolitan areas experienced statistically significant increases in their suburban poverty rates between 2000 and 2010.[2] By far the largest increases occurred in the Midwest and South, reflecting a mix of long-running and acute economic hardships that affected these regions over the decade (see table 2-1). Explored in more detail in the next chapter, the economic forces that

Table 2-2. Highest and Lowest Suburban Poverty Rates, 2010
Percent

Highest suburban poverty rates		Lowest suburban poverty rates	
Metropolitan area[a]	2010	Metropolitan area	2010
El Paso, Tex.	36.4	Omaha, Neb.-Iowa	7.8
McAllen, Tex.	35.4	Hartford, Conn.	7.8
Fresno, Calif.	23.1	Minneapolis-St. Paul, Minn.–Wis.	7.6
Bakersfield, Calif.	22.6	Madison, Wis.	7.2
Modesto, Calif.	19.6	Ogden, Utah	7.1
Cape Coral, Fla.	18.6	Washington-Arlington-Alexandria, D.C.-Va.-Md.-W.V.	7.0
Lakeland, Fla.	17.7	Milwaukee, Wis.	6.9
Albuquerque, N.M.	17.0	Baltimore, Md.	6.7
Augusta-Richmond County, Ga.-S.C.	16.9	Bridgeport-Stamford, Conn.	5.9
Stockton, Calif.	16.4	Des Moines, Iowa	5.7

Source: Brookings Institution analysis of decennial census and ACS data.

a. Metropolitan area names have been adjusted to reflect Brookings Institution–defined primary cities.

caused poverty to rise throughout the 2000s affected cities and suburbs alike, hitting midwestern metropolitan areas particularly hard.

Rapid increases in the Midwest notwithstanding, western and southern metropolitan areas continued to post higher suburban poverty rates than others (see table 2-2). In 2010, more than one-third of the suburban population in the Texas border regions of El Paso and McAllen were living in poverty. By contrast, and in keeping with regional disparities in the suburbanization of the poor and nonpoor described above, metropolitan areas with the lowest suburban poverty rates were primarily in the Midwest and Northeast. In the relatively prosperous metropolitan areas of Bridgeport, Connecticut, and Des Moines, Iowa, for instance, fewer than 6 percent of suburban residents lived below the poverty line.

Unpacking the "Suburbs"

Just as metropolitan areas across the country shared in these trends, a broad array of communities within suburbia, from distressed inner-ring suburbs to outlying low-density exurbs, also experienced rising poverty during the 2000s.

ACS data for the period between 2008 and 2010 allow us to identify 1,817 jurisdictions within the suburbs of the nation's 100 largest metropolitan areas.[3] These places are spread fairly evenly across the major regions of the country, though (as the discussion above might suggest) suburban jurisdictions that experienced statistically significant growth in poverty over the decade tilt more heavily toward the Midwest and South. Combining three years of surveys across different points in the economic cycle produces a somewhat smaller increase in the suburban poor between 2000 and 2008–10 (40 percent) than the 2010 data (53 percent), but the finer-grained look they offer is revealing.

Consider the three regions detailed above for their rapid pace of suburbanizing poverty—Seattle, Atlanta, and Chicago. Within metropolitan Seattle, many, though not all, of the steepest increases in poverty rates over the decade occurred in King County, in communities such as Des Moines, Kent, Burien, and Federal Way (see figure 2-8). To the north, in Snohomish County, the close-in suburb of Lynnwood as well as the farther-out communities of Lake Stevens and Marysville posted poverty rate increases of 4 percentage points or more.

As the suburban poor population in metropolitan Atlanta more than doubled during the 2000s, poverty rates rose by large margins in communities across the region (see figure 2-9). Over that decade, very dense, close-in suburban counties such as Clayton to the south and DeKalb and Gwinnett to the east of Atlanta experienced poverty rate increases of 7 to 8 percentage points. Rates also rose significantly in more urbanized suburbs such as Lawrenceville to the northeast, Canton to the north, and Kennesaw to the northwest. But some of the biggest upticks occurred on the periphery of the region, in low-density western exurbs like the small city of Carrollton and in Haralson County, and to a lesser degree in Dawson County on the northern edge of the region.

In the Chicago metropolitan area, poverty rate increases spread from inner-ring suburbs to the farthest reaches of the region (see figure 2-10). In Cook County directly to the south of Chicago, poverty rates rose markedly over the 2000s in older, struggling suburbs such as Harvey, Calumet City, and Chicago Heights. To the west of the city, the close-in suburb of Berwyn experienced a steep increase in the poverty rate, as did the farther-out and better-off jurisdictions of Carol Stream and Glendale Heights. Other previously low-poverty suburbs saw their rates more than double or triple in the 2000s, including Round Lake Beach to the north and Romeoville and Crest Hill to the southwest. Along with denser, older suburbs, many low-density communities at the fringes of

Figure 2-8. Percentage-Point Change in Poverty Rate by Jurisdiction, Seattle-Tacoma-Bellevue, Wash., Metropolitan Area, 2000 to 2008–10

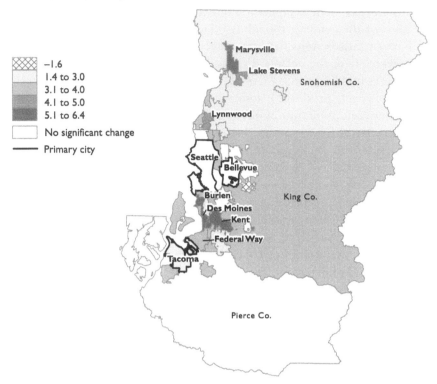

Source: Brookings Institution analysis of decennial census and ACS data.

the region experienced significant increases in poverty rates, including the city of Woodstock in the far northwest and McHenry, DeKalb, and Grundy Counties, which make up the western periphery of the region.

Broader trends within the nation's 100 largest metropolitan areas confirm that increases in poverty affected far more than the older places that animated prior research and policy development on suburban poverty. Over the 2000s, poverty increases in older, denser suburban places (in which more than 85 percent of residents lived in an urbanized area)—including Kent and Marysville, Washington; Lawrenceville and Canton, Georgia; and Harvey and Romeoville, Illinois—were matched by those in less dense suburbs—like outlying King County, Washington; Haralson County, Georgia; and Grundy County, Illinois. In denser suburban jurisdictions, the average poverty rate increased from 9 to 11 per-

Figure 2-9. Percentage-Point Change in Poverty Rate by Jurisdiction, Atlanta-Sandy Springs-Marietta, Ga., Metropolitan Area, 2000 to 2008–10

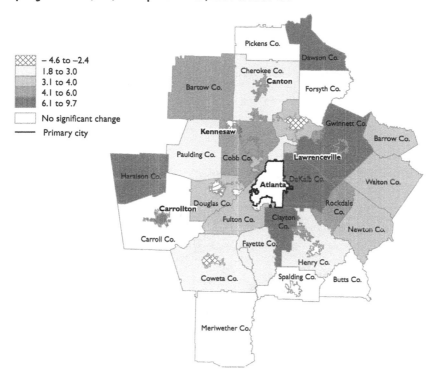

Legend:
- ▨ – 4.6 to –2.4
- ☐ 1.8 to 3.0
- ▧ 3.1 to 4.0
- ▨ 4.1 to 6.0
- ■ 6.1 to 9.7
- ☐ No significant change
- — Primary city

Source: Brookings Institution analysis of decennial census and ACS data.

Note: Data are not available for Heard, Jasper, Lamar, and Pike counties (not pictured) due to sample size limitations.

cent, fueled by a 39 percent rise in the number of poor residents in these communities. In less dense suburbs, the average poverty rate rose from 8 to 10 percent against growth in the poor population of 42 percent.

As poverty spread into more and different places in suburbia, it did not disperse evenly. In the Chicago region, for instance, especially rapid increases in the poor population occurred across a chain of middle-ring and outlying suburbs—places such as Northbrook, Schaumburg, and Elgin to the northwest of Chicago; Glen Ellyn, Carol Stream, and Aurora to the west; Park Forest and Lansing to the south; and outlying counties including McHenry, DeKalb, and Grundy—making them home to a higher share of the region's poor population by 2008–10 than at the start of the decade (see figure 2-11).

These shifts accompanied the emergence of a growing number of extremely poor neighborhoods in suburbia. Across the 100 largest

Figure 2-10. Percentage-Point Change in Poverty Rate by Jurisdiction, Chicago-Joliet-Naperville, Ill.,-Ind.-Wis., Metropolitan Area, 2000 to 2008–10

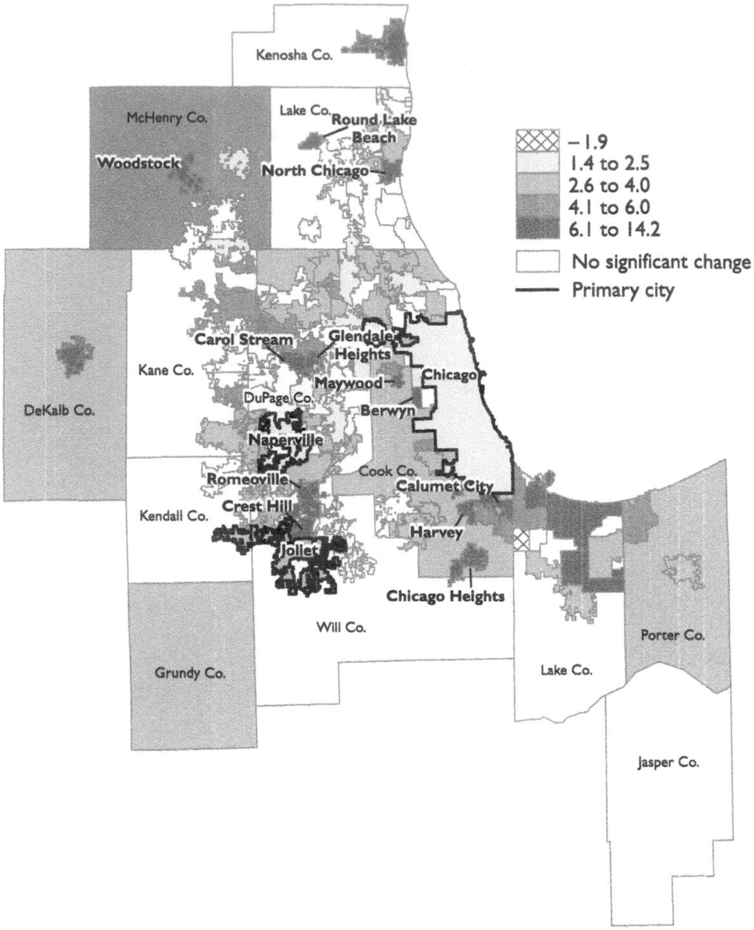

Source: Brookings Institution analysis of decennial census and ACS data.

metropolitan areas, the number of poor individuals living in suburban neighborhoods of concentrated poverty—where poverty rates exceed 40 percent—rose 63 percent between 2000 and 2006–10. This still amounted to only 5 percent of the suburban poor living in very poor neighborhoods by the end of the 2000s, compared with 21 percent of city poor who lived in such communities. Thus, while concentrated poverty remains much more prevalent in inner cities, more suburban people and places are beginning to experience its myriad challenges.[4]

Figure 2-11. Change in the Number and Distribution of the Suburban Poor Population, Chicago-Joliet-Naperville, Ill.-Ind.-Wis., Metropolitan Area, 2000 to 2008–10

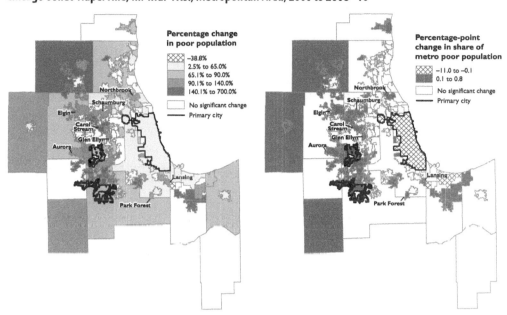

Source: Brookings Institution analysis of decennial census and ACS data.

Equally concerning is the growing number of suburban neighborhoods where at least 20 percent of residents live in poverty—a level at which neighborhoods begin to exhibit some of the challenges associated with concentrated poverty.[5] Fully 29 percent of the suburban poor lived in neighborhoods with poverty rates of 20 to 40 percent in 2006–10, up from 23 percent in 2000. Such areas could become communities of highly concentrated disadvantage if these trends continue unchecked.

Are the Suburban Poor "Different"?

Poverty's growing presence in suburban America often sparks questions about what, if anything, distinguishes the poor in cities from those in suburbs. In many cases, these questions stem from a desire to better understand a new and quickly evolving dynamic. However, they may also reveal the long-held perceptions commonly associated with cities and suburbs explored in the previous chapter—the idea that prosperity is to suburbs what decline is to cities. In this way, some might believe the suburban poor to be less disadvantaged than their urban counterparts, or that perhaps they experience poverty only temporarily or not as deeply.

In fact, the urban and suburban poor share a striking number of demographic and economic traits (see table 2-3). The share of poor residents who are of working age approaches 60 percent in both cities and suburbs. Very similar proportions—approaching one-half—lived in deep poverty in both cities and suburbs in 2010, with incomes of less than 50 percent of the federal poverty line. Poor city and suburban residents were also equally likely to work full time or part time, and roughly two in three poor families in 2010 had at least one worker, in cities and suburbs alike.

On issues of family formation and education, the differences that emerge between the two groups are relatively modest. A higher share of poor urban families than suburban ones were led by single mothers (50 versus 44 percent, respectively), though these households accounted for the largest share of poor families in both cities and suburbs.[6] Poor residents in cities were less likely to finish high school or go on to complete some college education or an associate's degree. Equal shares, however, held at least a bachelor's degree.

The largest differences between urban and suburban poor populations in 2010 related to homeownership rates and racial and ethnic makeup. More than 36 percent of suburban families below the poverty line were homeowners in 2010, compared with fewer than 20 percent in cities. Poor residents in the suburbs were more likely to be white than their city counterparts—44 versus 24 percent—though people of color were disproportionately likely to be poor regardless of where they lived. Overall, the racial and ethnic makeup of the suburban poor closely resembled the national distribution of the poor by race and ethnicity, with Latino residents accounting for more than a quarter of the poor population and black residents representing just under one in five. In contrast, black residents made up roughly one-third of the poor population in cities, as did Latino residents.

At least in part, these gaps reflect the legacy of exclusionary practices in many suburbs that slowed the ability of racial and ethnic minorities to suburbanize alongside the broader population and contributed to the concentration of poverty in inner-city neighborhoods, particularly among poor minority residents. The pace of suburbanization sped up among poor people of color in the 2000s: the share of poor minorities in

Table 2-3. Characteristics of the Poor in Cities and Suburbs, 2010
Percent

Share of poor individuals	In cities	In suburbs	Difference
In deep poverty	45.8	43.8	2.1*
With a disability	15.2	15.7	(0.5)*
Who are:			
Under 18	34.3	34.6	(0.3)
18 to 64	58.9	57.4	1.6
65 and over	6.8	8.0	(1.2)*
Foreign-born	22.5	20.3	2.2*
White, non-Hispanic	23.8	43.7	(19.9)*
16 years and older who:			
Worked full time, year round	8.1	8.7	(0.6)*
Worked part time or part year	32.5	32.6	(0.1)
Did not work	59.5	58.8	0.7
25 years and older with:			
Less than a high school diploma	35.8	30.3	5.6*
A high school diploma	29.4	32.4	(3.1)*
Some college or an associate's degree	22.7	25.0	(2.3)*
A bachelor's degree or higher	12.0	12.3	(0.2)
Share of poor families			
With at least one worker	63.8	66.2	(2.4)*
Who own a home	19.7	36.4	(16.8)*
Who are:			
Married with children	22.5	26.5	(4.1)*
Married with no children	9.0	12.9	(3.9)*
Male-headed, with children	7.9	7.9	(0.0)
Male-headed, no children	2.8	2.6	0.2
Female-headed, with children	50.0	43.5	6.6*
Female-headed, no children	7.9	6.6	1.2

Source: Brookings Institution analysis of ACS data.
*Difference is significant at the 90 percent confidence level.

the suburbs increased by more than 7 percentage points in the span of ten years, compared with an increase of less than 3 percentage points among poor whites. Even so, by 2010 fewer than half of poor minority residents (47 percent) lived in the suburbs, compared with more than

Figure 2-12. Average Neighborhood Poverty Rate Experienced by Poor City and Suburban Residents, by Race and Ethnicity, 2006–10

Percent

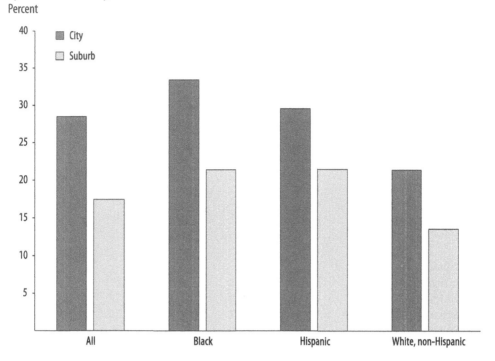

Typical poor resident by race or ethnicity

Source: Brookings Institution analysis of ACS data.

two-thirds (69 percent) of poor whites. Among poor residents of color, black residents were the least likely to live in the suburbs (39 percent), while poor Latino residents were more or less evenly distributed across cities and suburbs.

Just as in cities, poor suburban residents of color were more likely to live in higher-poverty neighborhoods than their white counterparts. However, consistent with broader findings on concentrations of poverty, the suburban poor experienced lower neighborhood poverty rates on average than the urban poor, regardless of race or ethnicity (see figure 2-12).

The biggest differences between the city and suburban poor—characteristics including household structure, homeownership, and race and ethnicity—may seem intuitive. After all, higher homeownership rates and shares of married couples with children conform to the suburban narrative of families seeking out communities with affordable homes, better schools, or safer streets, where they can raise their children. The racial and ethnic makeup of the urban and suburban poor differs, but reflects broader differences in the makeup of urban and suburban America that are themselves steadily changing.[7]

Yet in the end, it is striking just how demographically and economically similar poverty looks across city and suburban lines. Although these statistics may buck perceptions of what "new" poverty looks like, they underscore the fact that while places within metropolitan regions may differ, America's metropolitan poor share many common attributes and challenges, regardless of where they live.

Conclusion

For decades, the poor population in the United States has grown at a faster pace in suburbs than in other types of places. By the mid-2000s, the number of poor individuals in suburbs surpassed that in cities for the first time. The Great Recession exacerbated this trend, so that between 2000 and 2010 the poor population grew by an astounding 53 percent in suburbs, compared with 23 percent in cities. By 2010, the suburban poor population exceeded that in cities by 2.6 million residents. Over the same period, poverty rates rose by nearly equal degrees in cities and suburbs (roughly 3 percentage points), though the urban poverty rate remained almost twice as high as the suburban rate, on average, with differentials smaller in southern and western regions than in northeastern and midwestern regions with a history of exclusionary zoning practices.

Even as poverty regionalized over the course of the decade, it became more concentrated in poor neighborhoods. Although concentrated poverty continues to be a particularly urban challenge, by the end of the 2000s more than one-third of the suburban poor population lived in neighborhoods with poverty rates of 20 percent or greater. This signals that suburbs increasingly face the challenges of concentrated disadvantage. The nation may be at risk of replicating in suburbs the mistakes it has worked for decades to reverse in cities.

Underscoring the regional nature of modern poverty, poor residents in cities and suburbs—with minor exceptions—largely resemble one another demographically and economically. Though the history and development of suburban places may differ, in the end broader population trends, migration and immigration patterns, local housing market dynamics, and regional economic structures and trends have all contributed to the regionalization of poverty in the United States. The next chapter portrays how each of these elements—including their complex intersections in different regions—has yielded the new reality of suburban poverty in America.

3

Behind the Numbers: What's Driving Suburban Poverty?

The communities of South King County, Washington, inhabit the shadows of one of the nation's leading economic lights: Seattle. Yet some of the most intense demographic and economic changes happening in America today are occurring in those shadows.

The small city of Tukwila, located along the city of Seattle's southern border, exemplifies that phenomenon. For much of the postwar period, Tukwila was home to thousands of workers employed by the nearby Boeing plant or the Port of Seattle and its related warehouse industry. They and their families occupied modest single-family homes and small, garden-style apartment buildings characteristic of the era and the working/middle-class wages those jobs paid. As recently as 1990, more than 80 percent of this suburb's roughly 12,000 residents were white.

Today, Tukwila's population exceeds 19,000 residents and is a mix of ethnicities and cultures from around the world. Waves of refugees resettled

Tukwila, Washington: Stores and restaurants catering to Tukwila's growing immigrant and refugee population. (Kristin Johnson-Waggoner)

in Tukwila throughout the past two decades, including Bosnians and Serbs in the 1990s, Somalis and Sudanese in the 2000s, and Bhutanese and Nepalese after that. Latinos have migrated to the area from Mexico and Central America for work, some arriving seasonally from farms in eastern Washington. More than one-third of the city's population is foreign born. And in recent years, local observers note that in-migration from gentrifying neighborhoods in Central and South Seattle has accelerated, particularly among black families. By 2010, similar shares of Tukwila's residents were black, Hispanic, and Asian, while whites made up 44 percent of the population. Along the way, Tukwila has been transformed economically, too, as its poverty rate jumped from 13 percent in 2000 to 24 percent in 2006–10.

Poverty's rise in Tukwila is due in part to the advantages that drew working families decades ago. An aging and diverse housing stock and plentiful rental options make housing more affordable in Tukwila than in Seattle or the region as a whole. Proximity to employment hubs like the Port of Seattle and the Seattle-Tacoma International Airport remains an asset in a region where the bulk of jobs continue to move away from downtown.

As much as these attributes have paved the way for lower-income families and new immigrants to move to Tukwila, however, new arrivals and long-term residents alike have also confronted economic disruptions. Half of Tukwila's workers hold jobs in retail, hospitality and food service, warehousing, construction, and other services—industries that not only consist of lower-paying jobs but also were hit hard in the aftermath of the Great Recession. In the span of three years, suburban King County's unemployment rate rose from less than 4 percent in 2007 to almost 10 percent in 2010—outpacing nearby Seattle in both the rate of unemployment and the magnitude of the increase.

The phrase "suburbanization of poverty" suggests the movement of low-income populations into a new suburban landscape. Whether seeking jobs, affordable housing, safer neighborhoods, or better schools, struggling families move to suburbia from any number of places. As in the Seattle region, some make their way from the inner city to the surrounding suburbs, taking advantage of more affordable housing opportunities. Some move from other parts of the country, like the residents of struggling Rust Belt metropolitan areas who decamped for faster-growing suburbs in the South and West where jobs were more plentiful. Others move from states with higher costs of living, like California, to more affordable parts of the country, including Arizona and Nevada. And still others, like South King County's refugee populations, come from outside the country altogether. As Audrey Singer and her colleagues observed, "Immigrants have followed the suburban job and housing opportunities in great numbers. . . . Now many immigrants move directly to suburban areas from abroad," bypassing central cities entirely.[1]

But the phrase "suburbanization of poverty" can also obscure the full picture. Alone, it suggests that the rapid rise in suburban poverty occurred solely or primarily because poor populations pulled up stakes and moved to suburbia. While migration is certainly part of the story, a much richer and more complex set of factors has shaped the trajectory and geography of poverty, within and across metropolitan areas. While poverty has certainly suburbanized, suburban populations themselves have also become poorer.

This chapter looks deeply at three dimensions of change within U.S. metropolitan areas over the 2000s that help explain where, why, and how poverty has grown in suburbia: the economy and jobs, population and immigration trends, and housing.

The Economy and Jobs

One of the best predictors of poverty's trajectory is the health of the economy. Poverty and unemployment rates largely move together over time, and as economist Rebecca Blank has shown, the U.S. poverty rate remains very responsive to the economic cycle (see figure 3-1).[2] But while poverty rises with unemployment, its decline tends to lag behind improvements in the unemployment rate. In 2011, Brookings researchers Emily Monea and Isabel Sawhill conservatively estimated that even if the national unemployment rate fell to 5 percent within the next five years, by 2020 the nation's poverty rate will likely remain above 14 percent.[3] Thus, the effects of a downturn in the economic cycle can be felt long after it ends.

To understand how poverty suburbanized during the first decade of the twenty-first century, then, one must start with the broader economic picture. Although the Great Recession at the end of the 2000s looms large owing to its severity and recentness, the decade actually began with a shallow downturn in 2001 that lasted eight months and was largely concentrated in the manufacturing and information technology sectors.[4] Low interest rates and growth of the subprime mortgage industry buoyed the housing market and helped buffer the construction and real estate industries during the slowdown. Likewise, the South weathered this

Figure 3-1. Poverty and Unemployment Rates, United States, 2000 to 2010

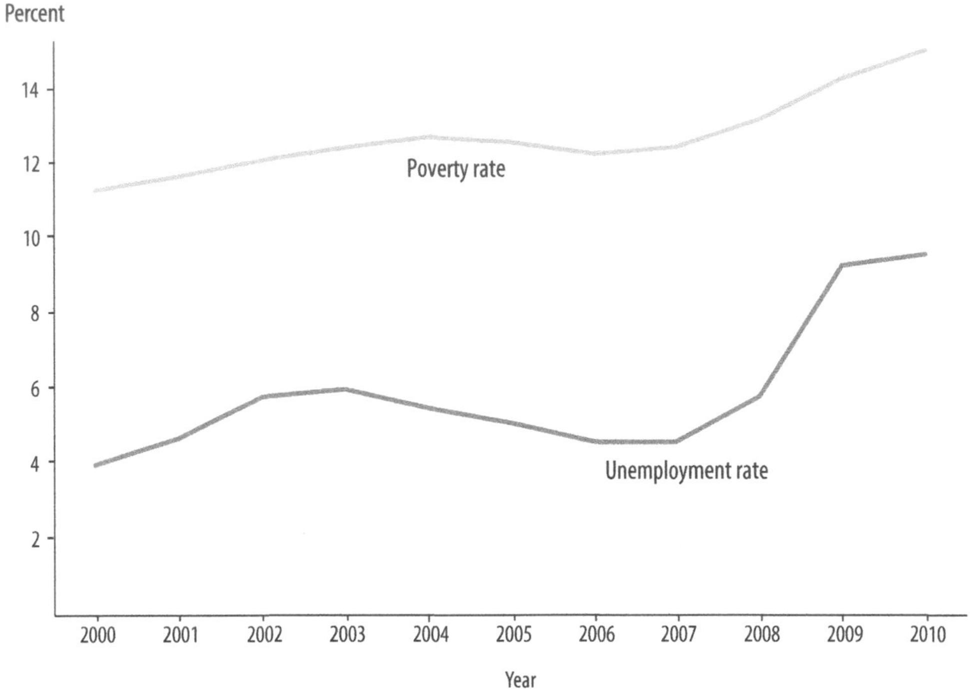

Percent

Year

Source: Brookings Institution analysis of U.S. Census Bureau and Bureau of Labor Statistics data.

period thanks to strong job growth in service industries.[5] The U.S. poverty rate rose from 11.3 percent in 2000 to 12.1 percent in 2002.

Emerging from this mild downturn, the country entered a period of so-called "jobless" growth. While the gross domestic product (GDP) and corporate profits grew after the official recovery began, nonfarm payroll employment did not reach its prerecession level until 2005.[6] The poverty rate continued to rise through 2004, reaching 12.7 percent before declining modestly to 12.3 percent in 2006. The stagnant poverty rate combined with U.S. population growth meant that, by 2007, there were 5.7 million more individuals living below the poverty line than in 2000.

The decade's second downturn, which began at the end of 2007, escalated into the worst recession since the Great Depression and left virtually no sector or region unscathed. It officially lasted for eighteen months, though job losses continued to mount even as GDP began to recover.[7] The bursting of the housing bubble brought significant job losses, initially in construction and real estate. Ultimately other industries felt the brunt, from consumer-oriented sectors including retail, leisure, and hospitality (which experienced record employment declines) to manufacturing.[8] Manufacturing had not recovered from the first downturn of the decade, and job losses only accelerated as the Great Recession deepened.[9] The U.S. poverty rate climbed from 12.5 percent in 2007 to 15.1 percent in 2010 as another 9.1 million Americans fell below the poverty line.[10]

Although virtually every corner of the nation felt the effects of the decade's two downturns, midwestern industrial regions and boom-and-bust Sun Belt regions suffered particularly steep increases in unemployment and poverty. In 16 of the 100 largest metro areas, poverty rates were at least 5 percentage points higher in 2010 than in 2000. Manufacturing-oriented metropolitan areas including Akron and Dayton, Ohio; Detroit; and Greensboro, North Carolina, never managed a full recovery from the decade's first downturn before the onset of the second, much deeper recession. In fast-growing regions like Atlanta; Boise, Idaho; and Cape Coral, Florida, poverty rates spiked in the wake of the housing market crash and ended the decade much higher than at the start. In addition, metro areas in California's interior—Fresno, Modesto, Riverside, and Stockton—experienced rapid poverty increases from 2007 to 2010 after the housing bust, reversing declines achieved earlier in the decade (see figure 3-2).

Even before the Great Recession, however, structural shifts in the economy were buffeting suburbs. Historically weak job growth between the decade's two recessions held back income gains for American families.[11] Between 2000 and 2007, median household income in both cities and suburbs dropped by roughly 4 percent—equaling a loss of $2,900 for the typical city household and a decline of $3,500 for the typical suburban household.[12] Among suburbs in ninety-five large metropolitan areas, fifty-eight experienced a drop in inflation-adjusted median household income during that time. The combined suburban poverty rate across all ninety-five metropolitan areas edged up from 8.5 percent in 2000 to 9.1 percent in 2007. As shown in chapter 2, by the time the Great Recession hit, the majority of poor people in metropolitan areas already lived in suburbs.[13]

More so than in past recessions, suburbs appeared to share the brunt of the Great Recession's fallout alongside their cities (see table 3-1).[14] Over the course of the downturn, overall unemployment rates in cities and suburbs rose by nearly equal degrees. In one-third of the nation's largest metropolitan areas, including Cincinnati; Houston; Madison,

Figure 3-2. Percentage-Point Change in Metropolitan Poverty Rate, 2007 to 2010

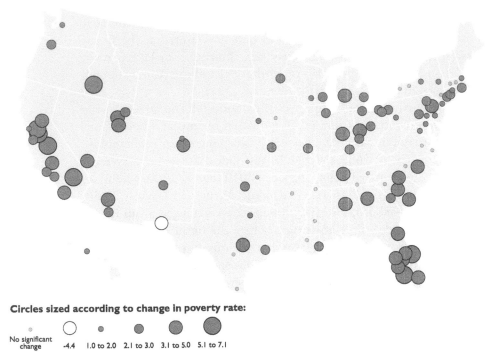

Circles sized according to change in poverty rate:

No significant   -4.4   1.0 to 2.0   2.1 to 3.0   3.1 to 5.0   5.1 to 7.1
change

Source: Brookings Institution analysis of ACS data.

Wisconsin; and Seattle, unemployment rates rose at least as much in suburbs as in cities. By the end of the decade, roughly 1 percentage point separated city and suburban unemployment rates, a narrower gap than at similar points after previous downturns (1.7 percentage points in March 2003 and 2.2 percentage points in July 1992).[15] Poverty trends in cities and suburbs tended to move together as well. Between 2007 and 2010, poverty rates rose by a statistically significant margin in the cities of fifty-six metropolitan areas and in the suburbs of forty-five metropolitan areas, with thirty-two metropolitan areas posting significant increases in both city and suburban poverty rates.

In part, the impact of the Great Recession on unemployment and poverty in suburbs reflected the downturn's suburban-led nature. Manufacturing and construction not only lost the most jobs among major industries between 2007 and 2010 but also were among the most suburbanized. More than 50 percent of jobs in construction and manufacturing were located more than ten miles away from major metropolitan

Table 3-1. City and Suburban Unemployment Rates, December 2007 to December 2010
Percent

	2007	2008	2009	2010
Nation	4.8	7.1	9.7	9.1
Cities	5.1	7.6	10.3	9.8
Suburbs	4.5	6.8	9.3	8.9

Source: Brookings Institution analysis of Bureau of Labor Statistics data.

downtowns in 2007 (see figure 3-3).[16] By contrast, smaller shares of jobs in less affected industries like education (32 percent) and health services (39 percent) were located at least that far from the urban core.

Suburban jobs and suburban poverty increasingly coincide in an economy with significant numbers of working poor. The share of Americans who were in the labor force for more than half the year but had incomes below the poverty line rose from 4.7 percent in 2000 to 7.2

Figure 3-3. Job Location and Employment Change for Selected Industries within Thirty-Five Miles of Downtown, 2007 to 2010
Industry

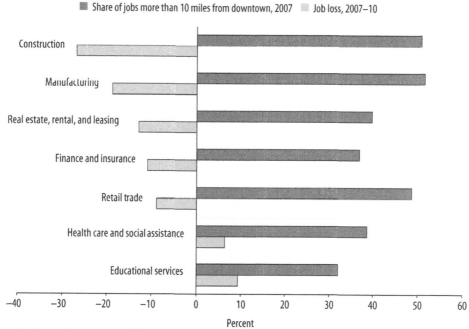

Source: Brookings Institution analysis of ZIP Business Patterns data.

percent in 2010.[17] Meanwhile, over the course of that decade almost every major metropolitan area and industry saw jobs move away from the urban core toward the outer suburbs.[18] Steven Raphael and Michael Stoll found that metro areas with high degrees of "job sprawl," particularly southern and western regions like Atlanta and Riverside, had more suburbanized poor populations.[19] However, the overall metropolitan population is more likely than the poor population specifically to "sprawl" in response to job decentralization. Raphael and Stoll suggested that other factors may still prevent some low-income, and especially minority, residents from following jobs to the suburbs.

Will suburban poverty decline significantly as the economy improves? Two trends suggest otherwise. First, the steady suburbanization of jobs is likely to continue, leading to more low-wage and low-skill workers residing in suburban communities. Although the Great Recession dealt a blow to many outer suburban communities, the decentralization of jobs seems only to have stalled from 2007 to 2010; it has not reversed course.[20] Second, more recent job gains and future job projections are concentrated in lower-paying sectors. The National Employment Law Project found that while middle-wage jobs accounted for 60 percent of job losses during the recession, they contributed only 22 percent of job growth during the recovery. At the same time, low-wage jobs made up just 21 percent of jobs lost during the downturn but 58 percent of the recovery's gains.[21] The growth of low-wage work is likely to continue, as economists project some of the largest absolute job gains over the next several years in occupations such as home health aide, retail clerk, cashier, food service worker, and child care provider—jobs that pay a typical yearly income around $20,000 or less.[22] Together, these factors suggest that poverty in the suburbs will remain a long-standing challenge for regions across the country, even as the worst effects of the Great Recession subside.

Population and Immigration

Just as jobs continued to suburbanize amid the booms and busts of the 2000s, so too did people. As in decades past, the population grew faster in suburbs than in cities and brought greater diversity to suburbia, both socially and economically. Overall, populations in suburbs in the nation's 100 largest metropolitan areas grew by 14 percent between 2000 and 2010—almost three times as fast as cities (5 percent) and faster than the nation as a whole (10 percent).

Notwithstanding this suburban advantage, significant regional disparities characterized population growth over the decade. As William Frey noted, in the 2000s "there remain[ed] a broad Sun Belt–Snow Belt divide in growth patterns for the nation's major metropolitan areas," mirroring regional economic trends over the decade.[23] These regional differences come through strongly in our sample of 1,817 suburban jurisdictions. Three-quarters of suburbs with faster-than-average population growth in the 2000s (468 of 628) were in the South and West—in metropolitan areas including Atlanta, Dallas, Houston, Phoenix, and Riverside. Almost two-thirds of slower-growing or declining suburbs (786 of 1,189) were in the Northeast and Midwest—in metropolitan areas like Cleveland, Detroit, Philadelphia, Pittsburgh, and St. Louis.

Yet poverty grew in all types of suburbs during the 2000s regardless of population trajectory. Combined poverty rates rose by 2 percentage points across suburban jurisdictions with both above-average and below-average population growth rates from 2000 to 2008–10. Increasing poverty accompanied expanding, stagnating, and contracting suburban populations alike over the decade.

In slow-growing and shrinking suburban communities, the combined overall poverty rate increased from 8 to 10 percent from 2000 to 2008–10. For some of these communities—like the Chicago suburb of Harvey and Shaker Heights and Garfield Heights outside Cleveland—as total population ebbed, the number of people in poverty stayed the same, resulting in a higher poverty rate at the end of the decade. In most, however, the number of poor people increased faster than the overall population (for example, Burien and Federal Way south of Seattle) or rose even as the population dropped (for example, Euclid and Cleveland Heights on Cleveland's east side and Oak Park, Eastpointe, and St. Clair Shores on Detroit's north side).

In suburbs growing faster than average, the poor population increased even more rapidly than the total population over the decade. That led the combined poverty rate for these communities to rise from 9 to 11 percent between 2000 and 2008–10. Many of these communities were in "bubble" economies like metropolitan Phoenix (for example, Chandler, Gilbert, and Peoria) and Orlando (for example, St. Cloud and Oviedo), regions that benefited from the mid-decade housing boom but were hit hard by the crash.

Demographic trends also contributed to poverty increases in fast-growing suburbs. Families with children and larger households, which are more likely to experience poverty, helped drive the suburban population increase in regions like Riverside and Atlanta.[24] Over the course of the decade, growth in the number of families with children accounted for roughly one-quarter of the increase in suburban households in both Atlanta and Riverside—more than twice the average for suburbs nation-wide (12 percent). In 2010, families with children made up 35 and 38 per-cent of suburban households in those respective regions (the rate across all suburbs was 32 percent).[25] Overall, children accounted for more than one-third (35 percent) of the rise in the suburban poor population during the 2000s, and 27 percent in cities.

These trends also reflect shifting patterns of location among immi-grant populations, who increasingly made their way to the suburbs in recent years. The presence of immigrants defined many central-city neighborhoods across the country for much of the twentieth century, from New York's Lower East Side to Chicago's Pilsen and San Fran-cisco's Chinatown. Today, however, 51 percent of all immigrants live in suburban locales, while 33 percent live in cities. Booming suburban economies have drawn immigrants and native-born residents alike, while slower-growing regions with longer-standing immigrant enclaves and social networks continued to attract immigrants. Refugee resettle-ment meanwhile shifted toward smaller cities and suburbs, like those in the Seattle region's South King County, to avoid overburdening local social service agencies.[26]

Because poverty rates tend to be higher among the foreign-born pop-ulation, immigration has played a role in the suburbanization of poverty. Roberto Suro and his colleagues found that in the suburbs of the nation's largest metropolitan areas, 10 percent of native-born resi-dents and 14 percent of foreign-born residents were poor in 2009.[27] Among the suburban poor in that year, one in five was foreign born. Suro and his colleagues pointed to different factors that may explain the gap between foreign-born and native-born poverty rates in the suburbs, like limited English proficiency and a lack of familiarity with the local labor market among newly arrived immigrants, and lower levels of edu-cational attainment.

While elevated levels of poverty in suburbia are due in part to the growing presence of new immigrants, native-born residents drove much of the growth in suburban poverty during the 2000s. Between 2000 and 2009, amid widespread poverty increases, the poverty rate for foreign-born individuals across all suburbs remained unchanged. In contrast, the suburban poverty rate for native-born residents climbed 2 percent-age points. Overall, the foreign born contributed 30 percent to total

Figure 3-4. Immigrant Share of Growth in the Suburban Poor Population, Selected Metropolitan Areas, 2000 to 2009

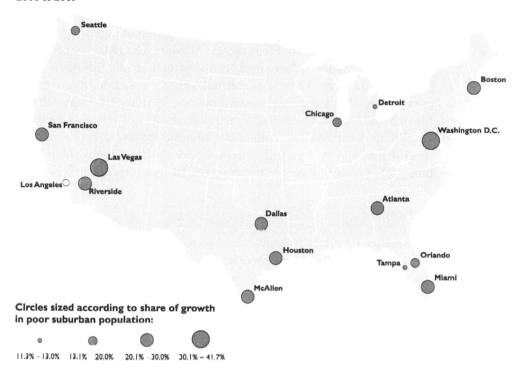

Circles sized according to share of growth in poor suburban population:

11.3% – 13.0%   13.1% – 20.0%   20.1% – 30.0%   30.1% – 41.7%

Source: Roberto Suro, Jill H. Wilson, and Audrey Singer, "Immigration and Poverty in America's Suburbs," Metropolitan Opportunity Series 18 (Washington: Brookings Institution, 2011).

a. The sixteen metro areas shown on the map had both statistically reliable data on the number of immigrant poor living in the suburbs in 2009 and experienced statistically significant (90% confidence level) change in the number of immigrant poor living in the suburbs between 2000 and 2009.

b. Los Angeles experienced a decrease in poor population due to loss of immigrant poor.

suburban population growth, but just 17 percent to the growth of the poor population in suburbia.[28] Immigration's varied impact on growing suburban poverty in the 2000s stands at odds with the perceptions of some local leaders, who lay the responsibility for rising poverty squarely at the feet of new Americans.[29] This may be due in part to the visibility of struggling new foreign populations and the relative invisibility of increased needs among longtime residents.

To be sure, immigration is a bigger piece of the suburban poverty puzzle in some regions than in others (see figure 3-4). For instance, in metropolitan Detroit and Tampa, immigrants accounted for only a fraction of the growth in suburban poverty during the 2000s (11 and 13 percent, respectively). Expanding poverty in those suburbs was attributable primarily to the declining economic circumstances of native-born workers and families amid the housing bust (Tampa) and manufacturing decline (Detroit). In metropolitan Houston and Washington, D.C., by contrast, foreign-born residents drove more of the growth in the suburban poor population (29 and 42 percent, respectively). Those booming regions attracted significant numbers of new low-income immigrants, many from Mexico and Central America, to their suburbs for jobs in construction, retail, and other services. And at the community level, the immigrant contribution may be even higher, as in the South King County suburbs of Burien (37 percent), Kent (37 percent), and Renton (56 percent).

Housing

Housing continuously reshapes the geography of poverty in complicated ways. Over the past decade, three housing-related factors contributed to the suburbanization of poverty, in varying magnitudes in different parts of the country. These factors included changes in the age and relative affordability of suburban housing, the distribution of affordable housing subsidies, and the housing market crash and ensuing foreclosure crisis.

Simple economics dictates that poor families will locate in places that have less expensive housing. In some suburban communities, especially in the Midwest and Northeast, the postwar suburban housing stock is aging and becoming less sought after and more affordable over time. This is especially true in regions where new housing stock continues to be built at the metropolitan fringe. The result is what Thomas Bier called the "filtering" process in real estate markets, where the movement toward newer housing leaves less desirable housing available for lower-income occupants.[30]

Many older regions are home to suburban communities characterized by an aging housing stock. In suburbs like Webster Groves outside St. Louis or Penn Hills in suburban Pittsburgh, upward of 80 percent of units were built before 1970. Many of those units are not the desirable, stately older homes that one can find in some city neighborhoods and wealthy suburban enclaves, but instead are modest postwar single-family and multifamily dwellings, once occupied by the working and middle classes. The limited appeal of those units in today's marketplace in turn makes them more affordable for lower-income households. Similarly, more than 90 percent of the homes in suburban Cleveland's Lakewood community were built in the 1960s or earlier. The city's affluent neighborhoods along Lake Erie contain streets lined with large, historic homes, but they lie a short distance from the aging duplexes and apartment buildings, many of which are rental units, that account for two-thirds of the community's housing stock and increasingly provide affordable suburban options. Even in a younger region like Seattle, Tukwila's small homes and garden-style apartments are about eight years older than the metrowide average.

A less widespread but critically important affordability factor in other markets concerns migration from cities to suburbs in response to housing price pressures. This gentrification is occurring in economically healthier metropolitan areas where city neighborhoods are enjoying renewed vitality and becoming less affordable to low-income households. In the Seattle region, for instance, rising housing prices in redeveloping Central and South Seattle neighborhoods coincided with the outflow of lower-income African Americans into South King County suburbs.[31] While the growing city of Seattle added fewer than 1,000 black residents during the 2000s, suburban King County added more than 20,000. These changes occurred as Seattle rents rose faster than rents in the surrounding suburbs. From 2007 to 2010, the typical Seattle rent increased 7 percent, versus 5 percent in the rest of King County.

Other economically buoyant cities exhibit similar dynamics. In the Washington, D.C., area, the typical rent in the region's major cities (Washington, D.C., and Arlington and Alexandria, Virginia) increased 38 percent from 2000 to 2010, faster than in the suburbs (21 percent). Brooke DeRenzis found that, amid rising housing costs in the early to mid-2000s, lower-income residents moving out of the District of Columbia between 2000 and 2005 were most likely to head into neighboring Prince George's County, Maryland, where housing prices were lower than in other nearby suburbs and housing options were better suited to larger households.[32] In Atlanta, redevelopment and revitalization of core neighborhoods such as Old Fourth Ward, Kirkwood, and Edgewood to the east of downtown, and West End, Capitol View, and Adair Park on the city's southwest side, helped spur rising housing costs in the city. Between 2000 and 2010, the typical inflation-adjusted rent in the city of Atlanta rose by 13 percent to $880, even as the typical suburban rent fell by 9 percent to $899. The increasing popularity during the 2000s of other cities like Boston, Chicago, and San Francisco among younger, higher-income groups undoubtedly contributed to the faster growth of poor populations in their suburbs, though the magnitude of that effect remains the subject of analysis and debate.[33]

The Atlanta region also exemplifies a second key trend that accompanied the increasing affordability of suburban housing—namely, the rising presence of households with affordable housing subsidies in suburbs. Nationally, the number of Housing Choice Vouchers (HCVs, formerly Section 8) in use rose 22 percent between 2000 and 2008. Over that same period, the number of vouchers in use in the 100 largest metropolitan areas increased by almost 400,000, accounting for more than 60 percent of the growth in U.S. Department of Housing and Urban Development (HUD) housing assistance in those regions to make up almost half (48 percent) of all subsidized units in 2008.[34]

Not only is the use of vouchers increasing overall, but efforts since the 1990s to increase their portability have also coincided with the suburbanization of voucher holders. These shifts took place as federal policymakers—concerned with persistent concentrations of poverty in very poor inner-city neighborhoods (often anchored by distressed public housing developments)—enacted a series of policy changes that helped shape the use and location of housing subsidies within major metropolitan areas. Beginning in 1992, HOPE VI ushered in the demolition and redevelopment of many of the most blighted urban housing projects, shifting many of the residents to vouchers (either temporarily or permanently) as the demolished units were replaced with mixed-income developments.[35] Just two years later, in 1994, the Moving to Opportunity for Fair Housing (MTO) program represented an unprecedented experiment to test the impact of housing mobility and mobility counseling on the economic, social, and health outcomes of voucher holders. The program assigned participants in five cities to three groups—those that received vouchers and mobility counseling, those that received vouchers only, and those that received neither—and tracked their progress over time.[36] In addition, a shift from certificates to vouchers opened up location options for recipients by removing the ceiling on how much a household could pay for rent, as long as rent did not consume more than 40 percent of household income. Finally, efforts to streamline the process by which recipients could use a voucher outside the issuing jurisdiction helped increase household mobility within metropolitan markets.[37]

In the wake of these shifts, Kenya Covington and her colleagues found that 49 percent of residents in voucher households in the nation's 100 largest metropolitan areas lived in the suburbs in 2008, up from 47 percent at the start of the decade.[38] Voucher holders are today considerably more likely to live in the suburbs than those living in HUD-subsidized properties, only 36 percent of whom live in the suburbs.[39]

In Atlanta, the metropolitan area experienced a marked suburban shift in the voucher program during the 2000s. From 2000 to 2008, the share of the region's voucher holders in the suburbs increased dramatically, from 66 percent to 79 percent—the second-largest increase among major metropolitan areas. The shift was also prominent in regions including Akron; Cleveland; Grand Rapids, Michigan; Phoenix; and San Francisco, where the share of voucher recipients in the suburbs increased by 9 or more percentage points. Depending on the region, a combination of push (high city housing prices) and pull (search for safer neighborhoods) factors likely fueled these increases in voucher suburbanization. Covington and her colleagues estimated that the growth in the number of HCV residents in suburbs could account for 23 percent of the growth in the total poor population in suburban communities from 2000 to 2008.[40]

These dynamics in the voucher program played out against the backdrop of a third important housing trend that contributed to suburbanizing poverty in the 2000s: the tumultuous housing market. A boom in subprime lending—including loans to borrowers with shaky credit histories and the proliferation of alternative mortgage products like interest-only loans and option adjustable-rate mortgages (ARMs)—ended in waves of foreclosures and "underwater" loans (in which the amount owed exceeds the property's value). Within the nation's largest metropolitan areas, 73 percent of the subprime loans originated between 2004 and 2008—the height of the easy credit era—were made in suburbia.[41] By 2012, the suburban share of all home mortgages originated during that period that ended in foreclosure also reached 73 percent, representing more than 1.8 million foreclosed loans, and another 1.8 million loans were seriously delinquent or in the process of foreclosure.

No major metropolitan area proved immune to foreclosures in the wake of the housing market collapse and economic downturn, but some suburbs suffered much more than others (see figure 3-5). All together, the share of suburban loans originated between 2004 and 2008 that were either foreclosed, in the process of foreclosure, or seriously delinquent reached 15 percent in 2012, nearly the same rate as in cities (16 percent). Some Rust Belt metropolitan areas had above-average rates of suburban foreclosures or at-risk loans (for example, Detroit and Grand Rapids), but most of the hardest-hit regions were clustered in the West and the Southeast. By 2012, 30 percent of mortgages in suburban Cape Coral were foreclosed or in foreclosure, with another 5 percent seriously delinquent and at risk of default. Rates were also high in the suburbs of other Sun Belt metropolitan

Figure 3-5. Share of Suburban Loans Foreclosed, in the Process of Foreclosure, or Seriously Delinquent, 100 Largest Metropolitan Areas[a]

Circles sized according to percent of loans foreclosed, in the process of foreclosure, or seriously delinquent:

6.4% – 10.0%   10.1% – 17.0%   17.1% – 24.0%   24.1% – 34.7%

Source: Chris Schildt, Naomi Cytron, Elizabeth Kneebone, and Carolina Reid, "The Subprime Crisis in Suburbia: Exploring the Links between Foreclosures and Suburban Poverty" (San Francisco, Calif.: Federal Reserve Bank of San Francisco, 2013).

a. The loans were originated between 2004 and 2008, and the map shows their status as of 2012.

areas, including Las Vegas, Miami, Modesto, and Stockton, each of which had foreclosure rates of roughly 25 percent, with another 5 to 6 percent of mortgages seriously delinquent. All of these hardest-hit suburbs also ranked among those with the largest increases in poverty rates between 2007 and 2010, underscoring the strong relationship between foreclosure rates and significant increases in suburban poverty over that period.[42]

Moreover, the impacts of the crisis were not borne equally within suburbia. Higher-poverty suburban neighborhoods (those with poverty rates of 20 percent or more) had an average foreclosure rate of 18.3 percent, significantly higher than suburban neighborhoods with lower poverty rates (11.0 percent). In fact, the foreclosure rate in high-poverty suburban neighborhoods exceeded that in higher-poverty central-city neighborhoods (17.9 percent).

To be sure, the relationship between foreclosures and poverty in sub-urbs is not a simple one. Many communities on the front lines of the phenomenon experienced a complicated mix of a cratering housing market, attendant economic dislocation, falling incomes among existing households, in-migration of lower-income households seeking newly affordable housing, and foreclosed properties. This interplay comes into view in the eastern Bay Area communities profiled at the beginning of chapter 1. Between 1996 and 2002, the city of Antioch, California, approved nearly 5,500 permits to build new single-family homes. Its population mushroomed by 18,000 people during that time, represent-ing nearly 25 percent growth.[43] According to the real estate firm Zillow, the median sales price of a home in Antioch skyrocketed from approxi-mately $200,000 in early 2000 to about $520,000 in early 2006. The boom was in full swing.

That boom showed signs of faltering by the mid-2000s, however. Homes bought as investment properties, often with high loan-to-value mortgages, ended up underwater as the housing price bubble began to pop. Owners began seeking out stable rental income, in some cases from lower-income households using Housing Choice Vouchers. Just between 2003 and 2005, the number of voucher households in Antioch increased by nearly half. Many, according to local experts, were African American families from East Bay cities such as Oakland and Richmond. Antioch's black population nearly doubled between 2000 and 2006, while the local poverty rate jumped from 9 percent to 12 percent.[44]

By 2007, the foreclosure wave started to ripple through the Bay Area, and Antioch was among the hardest hit communities. In the most strongly affected parts of the city with some of the newest housing, fore-closure affected approximately one in every eighteen homes that year.[45] Many renters faced eviction, and local affordable housing and homeless-ness prevention nonprofits were overwhelmed by demand. In parts of the city, when residents perceived that voucher households were causing problems associated with foreclosed properties, community tensions rose. The city of Antioch set up a special police task force dedicated to patrolling voucher households and Section 8 properties, particularly among the African American population, prompting a class-action law-suit that the city eventually settled.[46] Thus, the specific causes of subur-banizing poverty, real or perceived, can spill over rapidly into difficult consequences for residents and communities on the front lines.

Conclusion

The economic tumult of the 2000s—with two economic downturns, sluggish recoveries, stagnating or falling wages, and the growth of low-wage work and inequality—contributed to the decade's rapid rise in suburban poverty. Even before the Great Recession, suburban communities struggled with many of the same economic challenges that confronted the rest of the nation. And when the recession struck, the deep downturn was in many ways as economically devastating to suburban residents as it was to their city counterparts.

At the same time, suburbs continued to grow and diversify over the decade. Suburbs became poorer not only because long-term residents suffered economically but also because of the in-migration of lower-income families and new immigrants, many of whom were drawn by the continued suburbanization of jobs or the promise of affordable housing.

Whether due to job access, economic recession, immigration, housing market dynamics, or some combination thereof, poverty increases in suburbia are occurring against a diverse and complicated local demographic and economic backdrop. As the next chapter describes, what is in many ways a hopeful trend—the increased presence of lower-income households in once off-limits areas—has had uneven effects at best for many people and places.

CHAPTER **4**

The Implications of Suburban Poverty

On Pittsburgh's eastern border lies the suburban city of Penn Hills, the second-largest community in Allegheny County, Pennsylvania. Penn Hills came of age in the mid-twentieth century as a middle-class bedroom community for workers and managers at the nearby Westinghouse Electric Company, among other once-significant Pittsburgh-area firms. It is still home to Longue Vue, one of the oldest and most exclusive golf clubs in the region, once known as "The Millionaires' Club."

The challenges facing the region since the 1980s, however, have transformed Penn Hills both demographically and economically. In 2010, its population stood at about 42,000, down from almost 58,000 in 1980. One in three Penn Hills residents is African American, up from one in nine in 1980. The share of people in poverty rose from almost 8 percent in 2000 to 11 percent in 2008–10. The local unemployment rate, which was historically lower than the city of Pittsburgh's, now equals and

Penn Hills, Pennsylvania: A bus stop in Penn Hills, where transit cuts have reduced service to only a few pick-up and drop-off times during weekday rush hour. (Howard Davidson)

periodically exceeds it. Penn Hills is caught in many ways between its stable suburban past and an unfamiliar "urbanizing" present, facing a host of new issues.

Among the more pressing problems facing the growing low-income population in Penn Hills is access to transportation. The suburb covers nineteen square miles, has more than twenty distinct neighborhoods, and is traversed by an interstate highway, a few major state roads, and a series of local roads with only a few sidewalks that wind their way up and down the hilly terrain. Infrastructure in some parts of the township resembles that of a rural community more than a major metropolitan suburb. More often now, residents must navigate these byways without a car. By 2008–10, almost one in ten (about 1,700) Penn Hills households lacked access to a vehicle, notably more than three decades earlier, when the local population was much larger.

Public transportation service, unfortunately, is dwindling. Sociologist Alexandra Murphy profiled a predominantly black, low-income Penn Hills neighborhood where many residents have no car and many more cannot keep up with the expenses of the maintenance, repairs, and gas required to ensure that their vehicles run reliably.[1] One bus line serves the community but comes only a few times in the morning (into the city) and a few times in the late afternoon to early evening (back out of the city). As Murphy described, budget cuts at the Allegheny County Port Authority have left many more of Penn Hills's neighborhoods and residents with limited public transit options, including none on the weekends. These cuts have left many residents struggling to gain and maintain employment, particularly those working late shifts in the city or trying to get to jobs in neighboring suburbs.

Lack of reliable public transportation also complicates other tasks for low-income families in Penn Hills. The director of a local food pantry told us that many clients of the adjoining Head Start program had difficulty getting there. Residents without cars depend increasingly on family members, friends, or neighbors with cars to help them shop for groceries (the closest store is more than two miles from some poor neighborhoods) or get to a doctor's appointment, stressing already fragile relationships. A trip to get Women, Infants, and Children (WIC) benefits can turn into an all-day affair.

Penn Hills helps illustrate the paradox of suburban poverty. Ideally, the increasing presence of poor residents in the suburbs would signal that more struggling families are able to access better local environments with affordable housing, more job opportunities, lower crime rates, and better schools than are available in the inner city. In this way, suburbanization would provide them with a platform for upward mobility. And some poor suburban residents do indeed live in more opportunity-rich communities than their urban counterparts. Indeed, many lower-income African American families in Penn Hills moved there from very poor Pittsburgh neighborhoods or other declining steel towns that suffer even greater economic and social challenges.

Yet rapid growth in suburban poverty—in inner-ring and declining suburbs as well as in middle-class, affluent, and fast-growing communities—has caught many of these places off guard, exposing significant barriers to social and economic opportunity for their struggling residents. Some of the things that many poor city neighborhoods have—proximity to jobs, services, and transit—poor suburban communities lack. Other things that one hopes might be better for poor families in suburbs, such as better schools and greater safety, do not always materialize. This chapter explores how shifting poverty within metropolitan areas has affected families' access to many of the ingredients of successful communities, and how suburbs themselves confront different challenges in their efforts to promote opportunity for their low-income residents.

The Jobs Mismatch

Suburbs are where the jobs are. Only 23 percent of metropolitan jobs are located within three miles of downtown; more than 43 percent are more than ten miles from downtown. Moreover, the sectors most likely to employ less skilled workers—retail and wholesale trade, leisure and hospitality, personal services—are even more suburbanized than average. These trends might suggest better access to employment opportunities for the growing number of low-income residents in suburbia.

But that is often not the case. In many metropolitan areas, growth in suburban poverty and growth in suburban jobs occur in different parts of the region. Take the Washington, D.C., metropolitan area as an example. From 2000 to 2010, more than 40 percent of the increase in the region's suburban poor population occurred in just two Maryland counties: Montgomery (25 percent) and Prince George's (17 percent). Yet jobs declined in each of those counties during that time period, even as jobs grew in the suburban Virginia counties of Fairfax, Loudoun, and Prince William. With the exception of Fairfax, which accounted for 17 percent of the growth in the region's suburban poor, Loudoun and Prince William Counties experienced relatively modest gains in their

Figure 4-1. Share of Suburban Residents in Jobs-Rich Suburbs, by Race and Ethnicity and Poverty Status

Percent

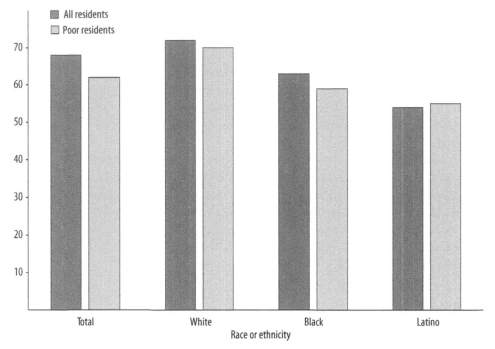

Source: Steven Raphael and Michael Stoll, "Job Sprawl and the Suburbanization of Poverty" (Washington: Brookings Institution, 2010).

poor population—capturing 6 and 9 percent of the rise in the suburban poor population, respectively—and no significant change in their poverty rates.

This example illustrates the broader trend chronicled by Harry Holzer and Michael Stoll that population growth tends to be faster in lower-income suburbs, while job growth is faster in higher-income suburbs.[2] As researchers Steven Raphael and Michael Stoll have shown, poor suburbanites are less likely than other suburbanites to live in "jobs-rich" areas, where the jobs-to-people ratio outpaces the metropolitan average (see figure 4-1). This is especially true for poor blacks and Latinos in the suburbs. The researchers note that the communities these groups inhabit "are frequently lower income and more disadvantaged—and potentially indistinguishable from disadvantaged central city areas."[3] Similarly, researcher Kenya Covington and her colleagues found that almost half of residents in suburban Housing Choice Vouchers households live in lower-income suburbs, while fewer than 30 percent live in neighborhoods with high job accessibility.[4]

A number of factors likely constrain the ability of poor suburban residents to locate in economically growing suburbs. Raphael and Stoll pointed to barriers in the housing market—such as a limited supply of affordable housing and the disproportionate share of public housing in urban areas—that may slow the ability of poor residents to follow jobs into higher-income, jobs-rich communities. Covington and her colleagues observed that those receiving Housing Choice Vouchers may suffer from a lack of information or adequate counseling on where better opportunities may be found in the region, and they may face landlord discrimination or limits on using their voucher in various metropolitan jurisdictions. Thus, living in the suburbs does not regularly translate into a job access advantage for residents, including the growing number with low incomes.

The Transportation Challenge

As the Penn Hills example indicates, the often considerable distance between the suburban poor and job opportunities places added importance on the availability, reliability, and cost of transportation in their communities. Indeed, transportation costs have taken up an increasing share of household budgets as working families balance access to affordable housing with access to jobs, which can often mean moving farther into the suburbs as families "drive 'til they qualify." In a study of the twenty-five largest metropolitan areas, the Center for Housing Policy and the Center for Neighborhood Technology found that households earning 50 to 100 percent of the median income in their region spent an average of 27 percent of their income on transportation costs and another 32 percent on housing, leaving limited room in their modest budgets for other necessities.[5]

Cars remain the most frequent mode of commuting for low-income suburban residents—74 percent drive alone and 12 percent carpool to and from work—but they can pose real financial burdens on those households.[6] Matthew Fellowes reported that just to finance a car purchase, residents of lower-income neighborhoods paid from $50 to $500 more than residents of higher-income neighborhoods for the same car, and auto loans cost lower-income drivers 2 percentage points more on average.[7] Although insurers may not legally use income or race to set rates, proxies such as education and occupation often lead to higher premiums for low-income drivers. According to a Consumer Federation of America study, low-income households paid 40 percent more on average for insurance from a large national company than more educated, higher-income households.[8] Beyond the costs of purchasing and insuring a car, low-income drivers also face frequent and costly repairs to keep the car running because they tend to buy older, cheaper vehicles.[9] In her field research in Penn Hills, Murphy found that many residents would go through periods with one or more cars out of service because of the high cost of repairs.

Notwithstanding the prevalence of automobile commuting in suburbia, 701,200 (or 5 percent of) low-income residents across suburbs in fifty-two large metropolitan areas rely on public transit of some kind to get to work.[10] Contrary to common perceptions of public transit in suburban areas, 77 percent of working-age residents in low-income suburban neighborhoods have at least one transit stop serving their neighborhood (within three-quarters of a mile).[11] Yet having a transit stop nearby does not guarantee regular or reliable service, nor does it mean that extensive routes and connections are available within the region. In fact, the typical resident of a low-income suburban neighborhood served by transit can reach only 25 percent of metropolitan jobs within a generous ninety-minute commute, and just 4 percent within a forty-five-minute window.[12] To be sure, these figures vary considerably across metropolitan areas, with low-income suburban residents of western places like Salt Lake City and Denver enjoying much better transit coverage and job access than their counterparts in southern regions like Memphis and Greensboro (see figure 4-2).

The vast differences across regions exist for several reasons. One is the extent to which metropolitan areas invest in their transit systems, and particularly in running service into far-reaching and often less dense suburbs. Those routes may not be cost-effective, and the coordination and funding may span multiple jurisdictions. For instance, although Atlanta and Washington, D.C., have similarly sized populations, Washington's extensive transit system linking two states and the District of Columbia serves its labor market much better than the relatively small Atlanta system.

But the amount of transit does not alone determine these outcomes. The ability of transit to effectively connect workers and jobs also depends on where people live and employers locate. In Chicago, for instance, ten local transit systems cover 91 percent of residents in low-

Figure 4-2. Share of Metropolitan Jobs Accessible within a Ninety-Minute Transit Commute for Residents of Low-Income Suburbs, 2010

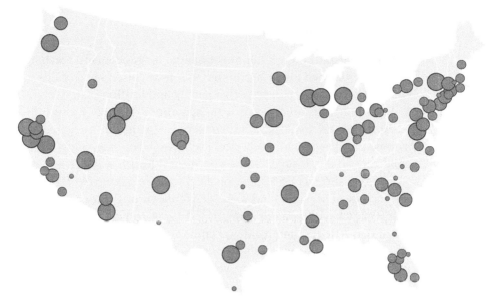

Circles sized according to share of jobs accessible within 90 minutes for residents of low-income suburbs:

1.4% to 10.0%   10.1% to 25.0%   25.1% to 33.3%   33.4% to 68.4%

Source: Adie Tomer, Elizabeth Kneebone, Robert Puentes, and Alan Berube, "Missed Opportunity: Transit and Jobs in Metropolitan America," Metropolitan Opportunity Series 12 (Washington: Brookings Institution, 2011).

income suburban neighborhoods. But a 90-minute commute connects the typical resident of these neighborhoods to just 14 percent of the sprawling fourteen-county region's jobs. Now that the region's suburbs contain more than two-thirds of metropolitan populations and jobs, and more than half the poor, the hub-and-spoke transit system originally designed to bring suburban commuters into and back out of the downtown Loop is ill-equipped to serve suburban residents trying to get to work in a neighboring (or distant) suburb.

Suburbs are also home to most of the low-income households who lack access to both a car and to transit connections. Overall, in the nation's largest metropolitan areas, 700,000 households do not have a vehicle and are not served by public transit of any kind, and 95 percent of those households are suburban.[13] Many live in communities that never had much transit in the first place or, like Penn Hills, have cut back transit in the face of fiscal challenges.

The Strained Safety Net

Reliable transportation is not only essential for residents to reach increasingly suburbanized job opportunities, but it can also play a critical role in connecting the suburban poor to a patchy and far-flung safety net.

Each year, the United States spends approximately $150 billion to $200 billion on social and human services programs targeted to low-income people—including services such as job training, adult education, child care, and substance abuse and mental health services—or roughly $15 to $20 for every $1 spent on cash welfare payments.[14] Yet because these types of services tend to be delivered through nonprofit agencies that contract with federal, state, or local governments, there is no guarantee that low-income residents enjoy easy access to them.[15] Instead, much of the scope and strength of the safety net available to poor people and families depends on what kinds of resources and nonprofit infrastructure exist in and around the communities in which they live.

As the modern safety net evolved over the past several decades, traditional urban centers were much more likely to attract and fund social service resources and infrastructure than their surrounding suburbs, in large part because that was where the poor were concentrated. As a result, Alexandra Murphy and Danielle Wallace found that at the start of the 2000s the suburban poor were more isolated than poor residents in cities from organizations that could help them meet their daily needs, and "even more so from those offering opportunities for mobility."[16]

As the poor population in suburbia expanded rapidly during the 2000s, many suburban communities lacked the fiscal and nonprofit architecture to respond to the needs of those individuals and families.[17] As Margaret Weir observed, because of the relative patchiness of the safety net in suburbia, "low-income people living in a suburban location—even a prosperous suburban area—with few social services may be at a disadvantage when compared to their inner-city counterparts."[18] Not only that, but according to Mario Small's research, communities without a well-entrenched social service network are less likely to have developed connections between providers that help clients overcome bureaucratic barriers to access a range of needed services.[19]

Of course, not all suburbs are created equal in this respect. In their research on the Chicago, Los Angeles, and Washington, D.C., regions,

Figure 4-3. Share of Large Municipalities in Suburban Chicago, Los Angeles, and Washington, D.C., with No Registered Nonprofits, by Category of Service, 2007

Percent

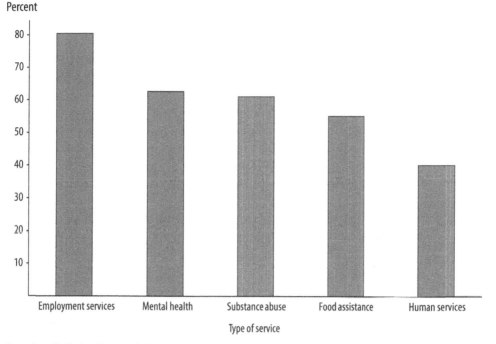

Source: Scott W. Allard and Benjamin Roth, "Strained Suburbs: The Social Service Challenges of Rising Suburban Poverty," Metropolitan Opportunity Series Report (Washington: Brookings Institution, 2010).

Scott Allard and Benjamin Roth found that the depth and breadth of services vary considerably across suburbs, with more limited services and resources available in the lower-income communities where needs are often greatest.[20] For instance, by Allard and Roth's calculations, affluent Montgomery County, Maryland, housed 135 registered social service nonprofits, which provided a total of $627 in human services funding per poor resident. In contrast, neighboring Prince George's County, home to the highest poverty rate among the District of Columbia's suburban counties, contained only 82 registered social service nonprofits that provided just $189 in human services funding per poor person. Moreover, the bundle of services available in the suburbs is often limited and variable across places (see figure 4-3). In the communities studied by Allard and Roth, 55 percent of larger municipalities lacked a food assistance nonprofit within their borders, and more than 80 percent did not contain an employment services organization.[21] In response, many providers try to fill suburban gaps by working in multiple communities, but resource constraints remain. Overall, Allard and Roth note, "the capacity and sophistication of municipal governments varies across suburban areas; not all have the size, resources, or administrative leadership necessary to be supportive partners for local nonprofit service organizations."[22]

Lakewood Community Services Center (LCSC) in Lakewood, Ohio, is one example of a capable but small suburban nonprofit organization facing unprecedented challenges amid rising local poverty. The agency offers emergency and supportive housing assistance for those at risk of homelessness, and it operates an emergency food pantry. According to Executive Director Trish Rooney, LCSC experienced a 140 percent increase in the number of people needing assistance between 2008 and 2012. Some of her organization's clients come directly from homeless shelters in Cleveland, but many others have moved to Lakewood from other, worse-off inner-ring suburbs or are longer-term residents who have fallen on hard times amid the region's broader economic struggles.[23] Many have serious substance abuse and mental health issues that neither LCSC, nor the city as a whole, is equipped to handle. More than half of food-assistance clients have annual incomes under $5,000, the result of a weak economy and new migration patterns. Another issue Rooney's clients face is substandard housing conditions, the prevalence of which strains the limited resources available for housing code enforcement at the city and county levels. LCSC makes frequent referrals to other agencies who co-locate in LCSC offices to offer mediation, legal aid, and mental health services to LCSC clients, but Rooney noted that the level of need coupled with limited resources makes it difficult to "get beyond triage."[24]

The thin patchwork of the suburban safety net derives at least in part from the jurisdictional fragmentation that often characterizes suburbs in the nation's largest metropolitan areas. Delivering services across more than one jurisdiction means that providers must in turn work with multiple bureaucracies, regulations, and reporting structures. For large suburban providers, those challenges can be even more complex and multilayered, as in the case of one suburban Chicago provider interviewed by Allard and Roth, whose organization served thirteen counties containing 81 city, 212 township, and 321 village governments. Serving such a large and fragmented catchment area added significant administrative costs for the organization in staff time, volunteer hours, and travel expenses, and complicated coordination, tracking, and outreach efforts. Regional providers must travel to participate in community meetings, reach out to multiple elected officials at the state and local level, and engage in and collaborate across a wide range of places. This fragmentation in turn creates conflicts and competitive pressures for large suburban providers that attempt to balance the needs and concerns of diverse municipalities and community stakeholders.

Another reason capacity in the suburbs lags behind need is that philanthropy has yet to fully adapt to the new geography of poverty. In their study of philanthropic presence and giving in the suburbs of Atlanta, Chicago, Denver, and Detroit, Sarah Reckhow and Margaret Weir found that community foundations in the suburbs tend to be relatively new and smaller than their urban counterparts and have not yet accumulated significant assets to bring to bear on the growing needs in suburbia.[25] Across suburban communities in these regions, lower-income suburbs by and large had fewer resources per poor person to work with—posting both fewer grantees and grant dollars per poor resident—than higher-income communities. What is more, grant dollars for low-income services, already limited in scope given the growing size of metropolitan poor populations, for the most part skew heavily toward cities in these regions, even though suburbs contain the majority of poor residents in all four. While Detroit showed a more even distribution ($1.6 million in the city compared with $1.5 million in the suburbs in 2007), the ratio of city to suburban low-income services funding reached 4:1 in the Denver region ($6.8 million versus $1.7 million); 7:1 in the Atlanta region ($6.3 million versus $900,000); and an astounding 33:1 in the Chicago region ($39.5 million versus $1.2 million).[26]

Reckhow and Weir found that many community foundations face limitations on the extent to which they can engage in more regional or suburban giving because of the often narrow or specific geographic scope of their foundation charters. But inertia plays a role, too. They noted that the smaller share of grant dollars going to suburban providers "suggests that philanthropies are primarily following well-established channels for grant-making. In other words, foundations in these regions are devoting relatively fewer dollars to building new capacity in suburban-based organizations; instead, to the extent that foundations are supporting services for low-income suburban residents, it is often through city-based organizations."[27]

Against this uneven and limited patchwork of services in suburbia, demand for services rose sharply in recent years. Surveys of nonprofit organizations have found that upwards of 70 percent of respondents have experienced growing demand in each year since 2008, reaching as high as 85 percent of organizations in 2011.[28] As the poor population approached historic levels in the late 2000s, nearly three-quarters of sub-urban nonprofit organizations in Allard and Roth's study reported seeing more people who had never accessed the safety net before.[29] According to the authors:

> Forty-five (45) percent of nonprofits indicate that they are seeing more clients who are eligible for government assistance such as [the Supplemental Nutrition Assistance Program (SNAP)] or Medicaid, but have not applied for such help due to lack of awareness or concern about stigma. A survey respondent in suburban Chicago observed that, " . . . there is a new group of people who don't know where to go for help, they are newly poor and don't know what to do."[30]

Similarly, although suburbs are home to a larger share of poor households, suburban areas continued to lag behind urban areas in receipt of nutrition assistance.[31] In 2010, 46 percent of poor urban households and 40 percent of poor suburban households received SNAP. Put differently, while suburbs accounted for 54 percent of poor households in the nation's largest metropolitan areas, they represented only 50 percent of poor households claiming SNAP.[32]

As demand increased in these communities, many nonprofit providers experienced significant cuts in at least one key funding stream, including nearly half (47 percent) of the providers in Allard and Roth's study of suburban Chicago, Los Angeles, and Washington, D.C. In 2011 alone, close to two-thirds of human services nonprofits had to use reserves to cover the gap because of late payments from a federal, state, or local government source.[33] Moreover, reflecting the toll of the Great Recession on philanthropic endowments and the volatility of the stock market since, foundation giving (already limited in many suburban communities) fell between 2008 and 2009 and remained relatively flat through 2011.[34] Thus, several years after the Great Recession officially ended in 2009, suburban nonprofit providers continue to face increasing demands on their services in the context of strained and often dwindling resources.

Access to Quality Schools

Schools tend to inhabit the front lines of efforts to cope with rising sub-urban poverty, no matter the particular factors driving the trend. School leaders in suburban Cleveland, Denver, Seattle, and Washington, D.C., described to us how they were among the first to detect rapid demographic and economic changes in their communities. They saw increased enrollment in school meal programs, witnessed increased rates of mobility among their students' families, or accepted the first waves of new immigrant populations into their schools.

These experiences coincide with national trends of increasing poverty in suburban schools. By the 2009–10 school year, 2.9 million more students in the suburbs of the 100 largest metropolitan areas were enrolled in the free and reduced-price lunch (FRPL) program than in the cities.[35] Their numbers had increased 22 percent since 2005–06; the increase among city students was 8 percent. Suburban students remain much less likely to receive FRPL than their city counterparts (39 percent versus 65 percent), but the gap between those shares narrowed in the late 2000s.

Although suburban schools grappled with rapid increases in the low-income student population during the first decade of the 2000s—either because of changing economic circumstances of existing students' families or the arrival of lower-income students in the attendance area—those schools remain, in general, higher performing than those serving similar urban students. The typical low-income suburban student in 2009–10 attended a school in which 45 percent of students met proficiency standards on statewide exams. Although by no means a great score, it nonetheless significantly exceeded the 32 percent of students judged proficient in schools attended by the typical low-income city student that year. However, it still ranked much lower than the 65 percent proficiency score for the typical middle- or high-income suburban student's school.[36] According to research from the Furman Center for Real Estate and Public Policy, portable housing subsidies do not seem to provide a direct gateway to higher-quality education. They found that more children in households receiving Housing Choice Vouchers (regardless of city/suburban location) live near poorer-performing schools, as measured by standardized test scores, than low-income children generally.[37]

The national numbers mask considerable variation within and across regions in the pace of poverty suburbanization in schools and its implications for the types of schools poor children attend. In the Bay Area, for instance, more than four-fifths of the increase in FRPL enrollment in the late 2000s occurred outside of the region's three central cities (San Francisco, Oakland, and Fremont). In the school districts of East Contra Costa County, the share of students receiving FRPL jumped from 37 percent in 2005–06 to 50 percent in 2010–11. Moreover, low-income students in the Antioch and Pittsburg school districts performed well below those in San Francisco on statewide exams, and about the same on average as those in Oakland.[38]

In the slow-growing Pittsburgh region, by contrast, FRPL enrollment increased in both the city and suburbs by similar margins from 2005–06 to 2009–10. There, 81 percent of FRPL students regionwide lived in the suburbs, and they attended much higher-scoring schools on average. Yet in Penn Hills, where the low-income student population increased even as total enrollment dropped in the late 2000s, districtwide scores on state standardized exams for math were only marginally better than in Pittsburgh, and slightly worse in reading.[39] Being poor in that suburb does not seem to give children a significant educational advantage over their central-city peers.

Access to higher-performing peers is one factor that might benefit some low-income suburban students relative to their urban counterparts. But even "good" suburban schools face new challenges amid rising poverty. Lakewood High School just over Cleveland's city line (the border is less than one mile away) saw FRPL receipt spike toward the end of the 2000s amid in-migration and income losses among its existing families. Students entering Lakewood High from Cleveland city schools are often far behind Lakewood students at the same grade level. Like many suburban schools across the country where need has grown significantly in the absence of a robust local safety net, Lakewood has worked to provide an array of academic and support services for its growing number of low-income students. But the school district lacks a full-time grant writer to help it pursue money for programs and services its students need, especially in the face of continued cuts in state funding.[40] Even though Lakewood High enjoys strong support from its alumni network, and remains a school of choice for many families in the region, it is struggling to help all students achieve at high levels given the rapid changes occurring in the wider community.

Similarly, Foster Senior High School in Tukwila, Washington—where the cafeteria is decorated with the more than eighty flags representing the home countries of its students and where more than 70 percent of the student body qualifies for FRPL—seeks to meet the myriad needs of its community by providing an array of services before and after school. A unique public-private partnership provides wraparound academic support and health services to low-income students and families, and it helps new families integrate into an unfamiliar environment. Nonetheless, academic targets under "No Child Left Behind" legislation have proved difficult to achieve with many students who are new to the United States and who possess almost no English language skills, not to mention limited literacy in their native languages. These issues layer on top of the larger economic challenges facing local families, including low incomes, poor nutrition, and health concerns, all of which complicate the educational picture for children and put additional strain on already stretched school district resources.

The Problem of Perceptions

Beyond the very real challenges that growing poverty presents for suburban communities and families, outdated and inaccurate perceptions of poverty often add additional barriers to mounting effective responses to those challenges. Common perceptions that the suburbs have little or no poverty can have real consequences for how regional poverty is or is not addressed. Studies by Allard and Roth and by Reckhow and Weir found that a lagging understanding of the geography of metropolitan poverty affected patterns of giving in the regions they studied. Providers reported that charitable donations from suburban donors are often directed to urban areas because the donors do not realize the extent of poverty within their own or neighboring communities.[41]

Similarly, if social service providers are not fully aware of the extent to which regional patterns of need have shifted in recent years, they may not align their services in the most effective ways. One mental health services provider was surprised to learn that the suburban poor now outnumber the urban poor in the organization's region.[42] The provider questioned the veracity of the trends, as well as the notion that shifting populations within the region might call for increased service capacity in the suburbs. There, as elsewhere, the assumption was that suburban residents in need of help could make their way to one of the organization's existing urban locations. This perspective was at odds with the experience of a small suburban provider in the same region, who struggled to meet the mental health needs of a rapidly growing poor population and saw a growing gap between regional demand and capacity.

Local political leaders help set a tone that can either advance or inhibit a response to suburbanizing poverty. How they understand the various drivers of these trends—including who makes up the growing poor population in their community—influences that tone. Much like what Alejandro Portes terms the "context of reception" around immigration nationally, suburban jurisdictions can influence where low-income families settle based on the level and quality of services they decide to provide, and the support and partnership they offer the nonprofit community.[43] Tukwila, Washington, has developed a highly regarded set of institutions and programs for addressing the needs of poor and at-risk students, including actively helping to incorporate new refugee populations. Leadership from within the school district and city council aids these efforts. Some surrounding jurisdictions, in contrast, seek to discourage these populations from settling in their communities by not providing such support. Poverty is still growing in those places, in part owing to downward mobility among native-born populations, but their decisions may leave relatively accommodating places like Tukwila shouldering a disproportionate share of the resource burden associated with an essentially regional economic phenomenon.

Increasing economic and demographic diversity in suburbia can also raise concerns about crime and safety. According to criminologist Mark Warr, perceptions about crime are often out of sync with reality, driven in part by the outsized coverage crime receives in mass media.[44] Those misperceptions can extend to how crime, and its relationship to poverty, has changed within and across metropolitan areas over time.

On the whole, crime rates have fallen in both cities and suburbs since the 1990s, though they remain lower in suburbs. But as crime fell in the nation's largest metropolitan areas between 1990 and the end of the 2000s, cities saw steeper declines in property and violent crime rates than suburbs, and among suburbs, denser inner-ring communities experienced larger declines than less dense and exurban places.[45] As the gap in crime rates narrowed between cities and suburbs, and suburbs themselves became more economically and demographically diverse, the relationships between crime and poverty, race/ethnicity, and nativity markedly weakened. In fact, research suggests that had suburbs not diversified, crime rates might not have fallen to the extent they did, and in places where they rose, they might have risen more.[46]

The power of perception, and the problems that arise when perception does not match reality, underscores the importance of building a deeper understanding of the shifting geography of poverty and the broader drivers and implications of these trends. The dividing lines between urban and suburban, or between first-ring suburbs and exurbs, have blurred amid poverty's expanding reach. The shared challenges that accompany its rise now belong to a much more diverse collection of metropolitan communities.

A Typology of Suburban Poverty

As the preceding chapters have illustrated, the suburbanization of poverty has affected a range of places in regions across the country, from recent boomtowns in the Sun Belt, to struggling first suburbs in the Rust Belt, to working-class and immigrant enclaves, to bedroom community havens for the middle class. Although the economic trajectories of these suburbs may have differed, many of the same drivers and implications of regionalizing poverty have affected them.

Nonetheless, to craft effective policy responses, it is critical to distinguish among the disparate array of suburban communities that have experienced rising poverty in the 2000s. Two suburban communities may face similar trends and challenges related to poverty's spread, but the resources and economic opportunities available to them to alleviate their circumstances may be quite different.

For instance, communities with stagnating or contracting population growth and a growing number of poor likely find themselves at a resource disadvantage. As the tax base stalls or shrinks, how do they tackle issues like services, transportation, jobs, and schools? Fast-growing places meanwhile face their own challenges in keeping up with the needs of a rapidly growing and changing population. Both types of local dynamics play out within a larger regional context, where a healthy labor market offers many more opportunities than a struggling one.

For this reason, we distinguish among different types of suburbs experiencing rising poverty on the basis of two key factors: local population change and regional job change. These factors can inform the responses of policymakers and practitioners.[47]

—*Local population change.* Shifts in suburban population signal changes in the tax base and potential resources coming into (or leaving) a community, as well as changes in the potential demand for services. The combined population of suburbs in the nation's largest metropolitan areas grew by almost 14 percent between 2000 and 2010.

—*Regional job change.* Changes in metropolitan employment provide a broad indicator of how regional economies weathered the economically turbulent 2000s and the impact of those changes on people and neighborhoods at the bottom of the income distribution. From 2000 to 2010, data from the U.S. Bureau of Labor Statistics show employment in the 100 largest metropolitan areas declined by just over 1 percent.

Figure 4-4. Four Types of Suburban Jurisdictions That Experienced Growing Poverty from 2000 to 2008–10[a]

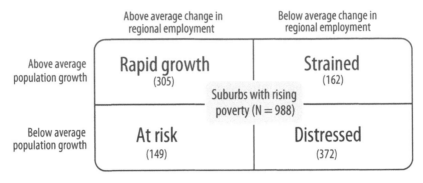

Source: Brookings Institution analysis of decennial census and ACS data.

a. Average change in metropolitan area employment between 2000 and 2010 was –1.3 percent. Average change in suburban population between 2000 and 2010 was 13.9 percent.

Of the 1,817 suburban jurisdictions for which we have data in the 100 largest metropolitan areas, 988 experienced a significant increase in poverty (whether in their poverty rate or number of poor residents) between 2000 and 2008–10. We divide the 988 suburban jurisdictions into four groups, based on whether they rank above or below average on these two characteristics (see figure 4-4).

Rapid Growth Suburbs (upper left) are those places with faster-than-average population gains in regions with better-than-average job performance over the decade. Taken together, population grew by 43 percent in these 305 jurisdictions between 2000 and 2010—more than three times the suburban average over this period—and the regions in which they are located saw metropolitan job gains top 6 percent. Their combined poor population grew by 71 percent, equivalent to 1.4 million more poor residents.

Several of these places are what Robert Lang and Jennifer Lefurgy term "boomburbs," large suburban cities of the South and West that have grown quickly in recent decades through the continuous addition of master-planned communities.[48] The Phoenix boomburbs of Chandler, Gilbert, and Peoria all qualify as Rapid Growth Suburbs. Each added tens of thousands of residents during the housing bubble, many of them Latinos and some immigrants, with plentiful jobs in construction and services. Many of those suburbs were also at the forefront of the downturn after the housing market collapsed. This category also includes many large suburbs of Dallas and Houston, such as Denton, Grand Prairie, and Sugar Land, communities that fared better during the recession but added many low-income residents and lower-skilled jobs over the decade.

Strained Suburbs (upper right) are places where population grew quickly but that are in regions that lost jobs faster than average. In the 162 communities that make up this category, population grew by 31 percent during the 2000s. However, their regions experienced net job losses of 5 percent on average. This category experienced by far the fastest pace of growth in the poor population, at 92 percent between 2000 and 2008–10, an increase of more than 622,000 people.

Many of these suburbs inhabit the so-called "favored quarter" of slow-growing regions, the portion that manages to attract new residents and jobs despite wider economic stagnation. Outside of Chicago, for example, the counties of DeKalb, Grundy, Kane, Lake, and McHenry continued to add population at a fast clip despite an 8 percent decline in employment in the wider metropolitan area. About half of these suburbs (48 percent) are in the Midwest, in metropolitan areas such as Chicago, Kansas City (Overland Park), and Minneapolis-St. Paul (Isanti and Sherburne Counties). Many others (38 percent) are in the South, including most suburbs in the Atlanta metropolitan area. This category of communities is the least urbanized on average (81 percent), with a higher-than-average share of newer housing stock (47 percent built since 1990). Immigration is less present in these places, with native-born residents accounting for a larger share of population (89 percent) than in the typical large metropolitan suburb.

At-Risk Suburbs (bottom left) are home to slow-growing or declining populations but are located in regions whose economies performed better than average over the decade. In these 149 suburbs, population grew by just 7 percent overall between 2000 and 2010. At the same time, jobs grew by 2 percent in the metropolitan areas in which these suburbs are located. The poor population in these communities rose by 46 percent over the course of the decade, equivalent to an additional 565,000 residents below the poverty line by 2008–10.

The suburbs in this category are spread across the Northeast (31 percent), South (37 percent), and West (28 percent). Many fall in the inner ring of suburbs in economically better-off metropolitan areas, such as Denver's Jefferson County, communities such as Burien and Everett in Seattle's King County, Pasadena outside Houston, much of northern New Jersey and Westchester County outside New York, and Montgomery County bordering Washington, D.C.

These communities are the most urbanized as a group (87 percent) and contain a higher-than-average share of multifamily housing (29 percent) and older housing stock (36 percent built before 1970). They are also more racially and ethnically diverse than the typical large metropolitan suburb, with 37 percent of residents identifying as nonwhite or Latino, and more than 17 percent of residents—including almost one-quarter (24 percent) of poor residents—as foreign born.

Distressed Suburbs (bottom right) grew slowly or lost population during the 2000s and were located in metropolitan areas with weaker-than-average economic performance. The most numerous of the categories, with 372 jurisdictions, the collective population of these suburbs remained largely flat over the decade (2 percent increase), while jobs in their metropolitan areas declined by a combined 8 percent. During the 2000s, the poor population in these communities grew by 52 percent, an increase of almost 1.1 million residents by the end of the decade.

Most of these suburbs are older communities with aging infrastructure, clustered in the Midwest (57 percent) and Northeast (27 percent). Cleveland's suburb of Lakewood falls into this category, as do Chicago's inner-ring Cook County suburbs of Berwyn and Harvey and Pittsburgh's Penn Hills community. Although not as distressed as their eastern counterparts, several older suburbs of San Francisco/Oakland (Alameda, Redwood City) and Los Angeles (Arcadia, Torrance) fall into this category given the net job loss in those regions in the 2000s. These 372 suburbs are more urbanized than average (86 percent), and more than half of their housing stock (51 percent) was built before 1970.

As the growth of the poor population in each category outstripped changes in the overall population, the share of residents living in poverty rose in each of these four types of suburbs during the 2000s (see figure 4-5). Rapid Growth Suburbs experienced the smallest increase in their collective poverty rate, at just over 2 percentage points. However, that category of suburbs began and ended the decade with the highest share of residents in poverty (12 percent). Distressed Suburbs posted the largest poverty rate increase among suburban types, from 8 percent in 2000 to 12 percent in 2008–10.

These four types of suburbs are positioned quite differently to address the challenges associated with their rising poverty. Suburbs with expanding populations will likely require different strategies than those that are shrinking. For instance, school districts in both the Distressed Suburb of Penn Hills, and the Rapid Growth Suburb of Commerce City, Colorado, outside of Denver are grappling with rising numbers of low-income stu-

Figure 4-5. Poverty Rate by Suburban Type, 2000 and 2008–10
Percent

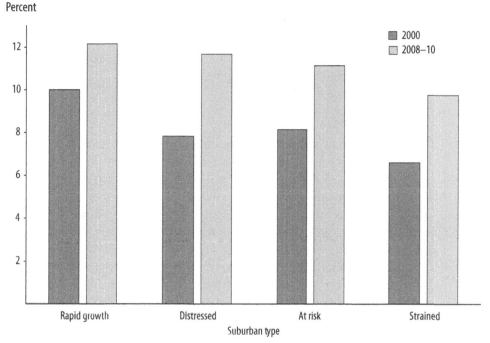

Source: Brookings Institution analysis of decennial census and ACS data.

dents. Yet Penn Hills does so against the backdrop of a shrinking tax base and a declining student population, which translates into fewer dollars to fund schools and maintain underutilized facilities. In contrast, space constraints and the continued influx of new students into Commerce City's Adams 14 School District, many of whom come from low-income families and have limited English proficiency, pose very different challenges for that district. It already relies on grant dollars to help make up the gap between its strained budget and the level of resources required to maintain a critical network of wraparound supports.

Similarly, the capacity to confront suburban poverty in economically strong regions likely outstrips that in struggling metropolitan areas. In the At-Risk Suburb of Pasadena, Texas, the poor population grew by 40 percent while total population rose by just 5 percent in the 2000s. The local tax base and municipal capacity may struggle to keep pace with the rapid rise in the low-income population, but the proximity to a growing jobs base in downtown Houston and in nearby refineries may offer pathways out of poverty, as well as middle-class population growth. In Chicago's Strained Suburb of Aurora, by contrast, the population grew by 38 percent over the decade while the poor population doubled. But the first decade of the 2000s brought net job losses in the region, reducing employment possibilities for low-income residents of Aurora, who already contend with limited labor market connections via transit.

Conclusion

The dynamics explored in this chapter underscore that suburban poverty is not a monolith, nor is it necessarily "better" or "worse" than urban poverty. Some suburban residents living in poverty may find that their location offers better nearby job opportunities or better educational options for their children than other communities. However, being poor in suburbia can also mean limited access to jobs, reliable transportation, safety net services, and the public will to improve these factors, complicating connections to the kinds of supports and opportunities that provide a path out of poverty. Moreover, local population dynamics and regional job trends intersect in ways that help shape the local capacity and policy options to address the rise of poverty in Rapid Growth, Strained, At-Risk, or Distressed Suburbs.

Although suburban communities may be differently positioned to confront poverty, the next chapter argues that they face common challenges in outdated and misaligned policies that address poverty and place in America.

5

Fighting Today's Poverty with Yesterday's Policies

Chicago, America's "second city," has been getting a second look recently, with the election in 2011 of its first new mayor in more than two decades, the emergence of more of its corporations on the global stage, and the 2012 reelection of one of its own as president of the United States.

For all of Chicago's urban muscle, though, it remains a heavily suburban region. More than two-thirds (68 percent) of the Chicago metropolitan area's residents live in the suburbs. And over two-thirds (67 percent) of the region's jobs are located more than ten miles from the downtown Loop. Indeed, many of the country's most iconic suburbs are found in Chicagoland—from the Frank Lloyd Wright bungalows of Oak Park, to the Northwestern University campus in Evanston, to the Highland Park settings of *Ferris Bueller's Day Off* and *Sixteen Candles*. All together, more than 280 suburban municipalities surround the city of Chicago.[1]

South Cook County, Illinois: A former Christmas-tree garland factory located between two areas prioritized for redevelopment around transit and freight shipping in Blue Island, Illinois. (Jodi Prout)

But Chicago's suburbs are a much more diverse lot than those examples suggest. To the south of Chicago, stretching into suburban Cook and Will Counties, lies a series of suburban municipalities collectively referred to as the Chicago Southland, including the likes of Blue Island, Dolton, Harvey, Lansing, Park Forest, and South Holland. The Southland thrived when heavy industry and steel mill jobs concentrated in the area to take advantage of the proximity to rail, shipping, and major interstate expressways. As manufacturing and steel jobs began to disappear in the 1970s, many of these communities experienced income declines and poverty increases more typical of the city's South Side than of its suburbs.

The recent housing crisis highlighted the fundamental misalignment between the Chicago region's new geography of poverty and the outdated systems responsible for confronting it. By the end of the 2000s, the Southland area was home to fifty-one foreclosure filings per 1,000 mortgageable properties—the highest rate in the metropolitan area, outpacing other suburbs in the region and exceeding rates within the city of Chicago.[2] But the relatively small size of many of these municipalities, years of economic restructuring, and sluggish population growth (or loss) meant that many of these suburbs did not have the capacity or resources to deal with the rapid spread of foreclosed and vacant properties threatening to destabilize their communities.

Recognizing these capacity constraints, the Southland suburbs had worked together since the late 1970s on issues that evaded the narrow geographic confines of each small jurisdiction. Under the auspices of the South Suburban Mayors and Managers Association and the Chicago Southland Economic Development Corporation, the suburbs joined forces around issues such as municipal management and planning, bond issuance and purchasing, brownfield remediation, public safety, infrastructure, and transportation. As the foreclosure crisis began to strike, they turned again to this model to access the first wave of federal Neighborhood Stabilization Program (NSP) funding—emergency assistance for state and local governments aimed at stabilizing home values in neighborhoods hardest hit by the foreclosure crisis. Communities in Cook County had two opportunities to apply for NSP funds—through an application to the state and to the county. Rather than compete with one another twice for critical resources, nineteen municipalities in the south suburbs banded together to submit a joint NSP application for more than $70 million in aid, based on a comprehensive strategy to link housing to public transit and broader economic development priorities.

Ultimately, though the state did not fund the collaborative at the time, the first-round NSP application attracted more than $9 million in funding from the county. However, instead of funding the collaborative, Cook County funded eleven municipalities directly, citing concerns raised by U.S. Department of Housing and Urban Development (HUD) technical advisers about whether the collaborative could assume the liability of a municipality and whether it could efficiently spend time-sensitive resources. But by funding each municipality separately and failing to engage directly with the collaborative, the capacity and efficiencies created by sharing resources and centralizing the application and reporting functions were lost.[3]

Although President Barack Obama's administration had repeatedly signaled support for collaborative, integrated, and regional solutions, the structural barriers inherent in a system built to fund states or localities (and not in-between entities such as the Chicago Southland Housing and Community Development Collaborative, as it came to be called) nearly scuttled the strategic efforts of Southland leaders.[4] One Southland elected official reflected on the difficulties he and his counterparts encountered as they pursued joint funding, stating, "We need new rules, because the current rules almost destroyed the collaborative."[5]

The idea of a cooperative approach to addressing poverty and opportunity is hardly new. When President Lyndon Johnson declared the War on Poverty in 1964, he not only pointed to the tools needed to increase opportunity and alleviate poverty, including "better schools, and better health, and better homes, and better training, and better job opportunities." He also called for a policy approach based on collaboration:

> Poverty is a national problem, requiring improved national organization and support. But this attack, to be effective, must also be organized at the State and the local level and must be supported and directed by State and local efforts. . . . The program I shall propose will emphasize this cooperative approach to help that one-fifth of all American families with incomes too small to even meet their basic needs.[6]

The fundamentals of fighting poverty have not changed since that seminal speech. Finding collaborative approaches that improve access to opportunities is as imperative today as it was almost fifty years ago.

But the shifting geography of poverty, combined with a legacy system for confronting it, has arguably made the goals of the War on Poverty even harder to reach. As the Southland example illustrates, agencies, programs, and approaches designed years, if not decades, ago to help cities combat poverty are fundamentally out of step with today's realities. Where poverty affects people and places in multidimensional ways, the system is siloed and fragmented. Where rapid economic changes and strained public budgets demand flexible solutions to poverty, the system is rigid and hinders collaboration. And where poverty is increasingly suburban, the system was built largely to address the needs of inner-city or rural communities. This chapter describes the current place-based antipoverty system in more detail, exploring the barriers it poses to approaches that more effectively confront growing poverty in suburbia.

Existing Place-Based Policies

The "system" to which we refer encompasses a range of federal policies that over the past several decades have evolved to alleviate poverty and increase access to opportunity in metropolitan areas. Though some may be commonly characterized as "place-based" and others as "people-based" policies, each has a spatial dimension that underscores the importance of place. (See Box 5.1 for a discussion of "place-based" programs.)

Building on a typology developed by Bruce Katz of the Brookings Institution, we group these policies and programs into three categories: improving neighborhoods, delivering services, and expanding opportunity.[7] Many are supported by funding or regulation at the federal level that is ultimately deployed at the local level, and several require additional matching funds from state, local, or private sources. As a result, the federal government provides much of the overarching structure of the current system, motivating nonprofit activity and leveraging state, local, and private funding around poverty alleviation efforts.[8]

Improving Neighborhoods

While there have been different iterations over the last few decades, policies to improve neighborhoods typically have worked to address the place-based market failures that contribute to poverty by upgrading the physical and economic environments in poor neighborhoods. In part, the neighborhood improvement approach emerged as a response to urban renewal policies that appeared in the 1930s and continued through the 1970s, which redeveloped distressed inner-city neighborhoods in a top-down effort to eradicate urban blight. These programs included the 1949 Housing Act, which ushered in urban redevelopment

Box 5-1. Place, Poverty, and Policy

An ongoing debate pits the benefits of "people-based" versus "place-based" policies in addressing poverty and disadvantage. People-based policies attempt to assist low-income individuals and families directly, targeting resources to recipients based on their income, labor market status, or family circumstances. Place-based policies target assistance to low-income communities in attempts to remedy market failures that may frustrate economic mobility for their residents.

The prevailing view of many economists is that people-based policies generally present the most effective option for improving the well-being of poor residents. Edward Glaeser has argued that people-based strategies are largely preferable to and more effective than place-based policies because they provide better-targeted interventions that avoid anchoring poor residents to poor neighborhoods. Glaeser stated, "We should focus on helping people not places, although we can continue to use some place-based tools, like schools, to help poor children."[a] Along those lines, Russell Crane and Michael Manville observed: "If the policy goal is simply to increase individual resources, then the standard critique asserts that place conditions are only second best. However, there may be instances where second best is the best available."[b] They noted that place-based policies may prove more politically feasible in a climate where government transfers are likely to be small or unstable, or when used to provide community-level public goods such as education or public safety.

Indeed, the debate between place-based and people-based approaches sets up a false dichotomy, often focusing on either/or when the application should be more both/and. James Spencer summarized this tension:

> The people-place debate diverts attention away from the development of approaches that simultaneously improve both people and places in favor of falsely binary people-place policy decisions. . . . After all, the intent of place-based policies—whether targeted at the labor market, schools, or public infrastructure—is to provide improved quality of life for neighborhood residents. Likewise, the effect of people-based policies can be highly spatial and place-oriented in its benefits, providing neighborhood benefits to non-program participants.[c]

Pitting people-based against place-based approaches to poverty alleviation limits the ability to leverage the combined benefits of these different strategies. In recognition of these overlapping effects, our discussion of the current policy framework for addressing metropolitan poverty and opportunity encompasses a continuum of approaches that rely either directly or indirectly on place.

a. Edward Glaeser, "Where Edwards Is Right," *New York Sun*, August 7, 2007.

b. Randall Crane and Michael Manville, "People or Place? Revisiting the Who versus the Where of Urban Development," *Land Lines* (Cambridge, Mass.: Lincoln Institute of Land Policy, 2008), p. 5.

c. James H. Spencer, "People, Places and Policy: A Politically-Relevant Framework for Efforts to Reduce Concentrated Poverty and Joblessness," working paper (College of Social Sciences Public Policy Center, University of Hawaii at Manoa, December 2002), pp. 6, 12.

(later known as renewal) policies and enabled the development of inner-city public housing towers in racial ghettos, and the 1956 U.S. Interstate Highway program, which is thought to have torn down more low-income neighborhoods than either urban renewal or inner-city public housing developments.[9]

In contrast, neighborhood improvement policies have adopted more of a bottom-up approach to addressing the ill effects of concentrated disadvantage, seeking to work within distressed neighborhoods to improve the lives of the poor "in place."[10] These strategies focus primarily on bringing better housing and job opportunities into poor neighborhoods, or working toward a wholesale transformation of distressed places into stable mixed-income and mixed-use communities. Bruce Katz observed:

> American-style neighborhood improvement represents an interesting blend of theories of community empowerment, corporate social responsibility, and market engagement. It applies a public-private partnership model at the neighborhood level. Nonprofit community organizations become adept at performing functions (e.g., building affordable housing, making home loans) that are normally carried out by for-profit institutions. They are financed in these endeavors, not only by government grants, but by private equity raised through syndications of tax credits, large-scale philanthropic investment in organizational capacity, and private-sector mortgage finance.[11]

Perhaps no one policy area illustrates this complexity and blend of policy vehicles for neighborhood improvement—from regulation to tax credits to competitive and formula grants—more than affordable housing. A panoply of federal policy tools seeks to increase the availability of affordable housing in local communities.[12]

—Enacted in 1977 to address redlining in low-income neighborhoods, the Community Reinvestment Act (CRA) requires federally insured depository institutions to meet the credit needs of the communities (including low- and moderate-income neighborhoods) in which they do business and stimulates private-sector investment in many of the other leading tools for affordable housing development.

—The Low Income Housing Tax Credit (LIHTC), started in 1986, provides an annual allotment of federal income tax credits to states, which then disburse them to private developers who agree to set aside a certain number of units for low- to moderate-income renters.

—Since 1992, the HOME Investment Partnership program has provided funds for the acquisition, construction, and rehabilitation of affordable housing through a formula grant to state and local governments. In addition, it requires recipients to set aside 15 percent of the program funds for community housing development organizations.

—HOPE VI, which also began in 1992, functioned as a competitive grant available to public housing authorities in areas with severely distressed units in their housing stock. The program leveraged public and private dollars to redevelop the worst concentrations of distressed public housing and replace them with lower-density, better-designed, and economically integrated housing options.

These are only a few of the dozens of federal policies and programs designed to increase the supply of affordable housing, but they demonstrate the range of approaches to this issue that aim to help low-income people and places.

Neighborhood improvement strategies also encompass policies designed to encourage community and economic development and to achieve better education and health outcomes for residents of disadvantaged neighborhoods. The Community Development Block Grant (CDBG) program, created in 1974, provides flexible resources to state and local governments for a range of activities that promote community and economic development. In addition, programs like Empowerment Zones, enacted in 1993, and New Market Tax Credits, started in 2000, focus on attracting and stimulating business investment in distressed and disinvested communities.

More recently, policies such as the Obama administration's Choice Neighborhoods program have adopted an arguably more holistic approach to revitalizing distressed areas. Building on HOPE VI, the Choice Neighborhoods program seeks to turn distressed communities and federally subsidized housing projects into stable mixed-income communities by linking housing improvements with access to services, schools, transportation, and employment opportunities, and emphasizing local community planning.

Altogether, the federal government dedicated about $14 billion in spending programs and tax incentives in 2012 to efforts aimed explicitly at neighborhood improvement. The LIHTC alone accounted for more than one-third of that spending, at $5.6 billion. Of course, this total does not account for the impact of important laws and regulations such as the CRA on the allocation of private capital to low-income communities. In addition, many of these funding streams, such as the LIHTC and

CDBG loan guarantees, generate significant private and philanthropic financial leverage not captured in federal outlays.[13]

Delivering Services

Neighborhood improvement programs are defined by a focus on helping to revive economically distressed communities and in the process provide better opportunities for their residents. A second set of programs seeks not to transform these communities economically but to deliver services to their residents. These "people-based" antipoverty programs do not necessarily address the place-based market failures affecting low-income communities (for example, inadequate housing or business activity). Instead, they help meet basic needs or provide support for low-income individuals and families that enable them to find and keep employment.[14] Because these programs rely on in-person, "bricks and mortar" delivery of services and benefits, they tend to cluster in areas that have traditionally exhibited the greatest or most concentrated need. The method of delivery for these types of services makes them inherently place based, as Scott Allard's research has shown, meaning that where one lives has a direct impact on one's ability (or lack thereof) to access this range of supports.[15]

Like neighborhood improvement strategies, service delivery programs and policies encompass a range of funding and delivery mechanisms, from broad block grants, to subsidies, to in-kind benefits.

—The Community Services Block Grant, consolidated from a range of existing programs in 1981, disburses federal funds to states based on the size of the low-income population. Much of the money is passed through to local Community Action Agencies—many established during the War on Poverty in the 1960s—to be used for an array of poverty alleviation efforts. The larger Social Services Block Grant, also established in 1981, is allocated to states based on population and then distributed to local providers of services for disadvantaged children and adults, as well as those facing mental health or substance abuse issues.

—For families with children, a number of programs exist to help families obtain child care and education opportunities. The Child Care and Development Fund, which emerged in its current form in 1996 as part of welfare reform, operates as a block grant to states to subsidize child care for low-income families and to improve child care quality. States use the funds to make child care more affordable by providing vouchers to families or through grants and contracts with providers. The Head Start program, established in 1965 and expanded in 1981, provides comprehensive education, health, nutrition, and parental involvement services to disadvantaged preschoolers and their families. In 1995, Early Head Start expanded services to children from birth to age 3.

—To meet basic nutrition needs, the Commodity Supplemental Food Program and the Special Supplemental Nutrition Program for Women, Infants, and Children (WIC) serve similar populations by providing healthy food to pregnant and postpartum women and children. The first program (which also serves the elderly) does so by providing food to state agencies, which in turn distribute it to public and nonprofit local agencies, while the second program allows low-income participants to claim food vouchers at a local or regional WIC office.

—For job seekers, Workforce Investment Act programs, delivered through One-Stop Career Centers, provide a range of services, including training opportunities, career counseling, and job listings.

—Community Health Centers (CHCs), created in 1965, provide health and social service access points for medically underserved areas and populations, including areas with little access to health care as well as uninsured, underinsured, and low-income residents. Unlike some other service delivery programs, CHCs are geographically targeted to places with high poverty rates and a lack of primary care physicians.

—Also geographically targeted, the Promise Neighborhoods program, modeled on the famed Harlem Children's Zone, seeks to improve educational and developmental outcomes in distressed urban and rural communities by providing grants to help communities implement a continuum of "cradle to career" services.

These service delivery programs vary greatly in size and geographic scope, from $16 million in grants to support access to farmers' markets for WIC participants, to $14 billion in Title I grants that supplement local school districts' spending on low-income children. Although identifying which people-based antipoverty programs have an important "place" nexus is inherently subjective, we estimate that the federal government spent roughly $48 billion on such service delivery programs in 2012.

Expanding Opportunity

Both neighborhood improvement and service delivery programs aim to improve life chances for low-income people by directly or indirectly focusing resources on the low-income places in which many of them live. Rather than tackle issues affecting poor communities themselves, a third category of policies seeks to expand opportunity by giving low-income residents of struggling neighborhoods a wider set of options—related to housing, jobs, or education—within their metropolitan region. Many of these strategies evolved over the years as part of the effort to overcome segregation in housing and education, to combat the deleterious effects of inner-city concentrated poverty, and to ameliorate the spatial mismatch between housing and jobs for low-income and minority residents.

—Efforts to open up housing opportunities included the Fair Housing Act, passed in 1968 as part of the Civil Rights Act, which made it unlawful to refuse to sell to, rent to, or negotiate with a person based on characteristics such as race, gender, religion, or disability status.

—As discussed in chapter 3, the growing use of Housing Choice Vouchers (HCVs) presented recipients with a broader array of location options than traditional public and subsidized housing programs.

—Related experiments that made use of the portability of Section 8 subsidies and vouchers, including the Gautreaux Assisted Housing Program (enacted by court order in 1976) and Moving to Opportunity for Fair Housing (a demonstration program started in 1994), tested the effects of portability and assessed the impacts on families of moving from high-poverty to lower-poverty neighborhoods.

—Sustainable Communities planning grants, initiated in 2010, encourage regions to more effectively align land-use, housing, and transportation investments to increase access to affordable housing and employment opportunities.

—Beyond housing options, policies like the Job Access and Reverse Commute program, created in 1998, allot funds to states and urbanized areas via formula (based on the share of low-income residents) to support transportation services that improve access to employment and related destinations—including training, education, and child care services—for residents of low-income neighborhoods.

—To improve education opportunities for families in low-income areas, particularly in major urban school districts, the federal Charter Schools Program supports the establishment of public schools that do not require residence in the surrounding neighborhood to attend.

These efforts to expand opportunity through housing, education, and transportation represent a smaller share of the federal budget than other antipoverty programs that aim to improve neighborhoods or deliver services in place. In 2012, the federal government spent an estimated $20 billion in this area, mostly reflecting the impact of the HCV program. This does not, of course, include the impact of laws like the Fair Housing Act or the myriad state and local programs designed explicitly to increase the supply of affordable housing in lower-poverty locations through subsidies or policies such as inclusionary zoning.

Table 5-1. Significant Place-Focused Federal Antipoverty Policies by Category and FY2012 Expenditure

Improve neighborhoods	Deliver services	Expand opportunity
Low Income Housing Tax Credit ($5.6 billion; TREAS)	Title I school funding ($14.5 billion; ED)	Tenant-Based Rental Assistance (Vouchers; $18.9 billion; HUD)
Community Development Block Grant (CDBG) Entitlement Grants ($2.9 billion; HUD)	Head Start/Early Head Start ($5.0 billion; HHS)	Work Opportunity Tax Credit ($0.5 billion; TREAS)
Supportive Housing Program ($1.2 billion; HUD)	Child and Adult Care Food Program ($2.8 billion; USDA)	Qualified Zone Academy Bonds ($0.4 billion; ED)
HOME Investment Partnership ($1.0 billion; HUD)	Improving Teacher Quality State Grants ($2.5 billion; ED)	Charter Schools Program ($0.3 billion; ED)
New Markets Tax Credit ($0.6 billion; TREAS)	Child Care and Development Block Grant ($2.3 billion; HHS)	Job Access and Reverse Commute ($0.2 billion; DOT)
Community Reinvestment Act (No direct expenditure; FED)	Consolidated Health Centers ($2.3 billion; HHS)	Sustainable Communities Regional Planning Grants ($0.1 billion; HUD)
24 programs, $14.1 billion	**49 programs, $47.7 billion**	**8 programs, $20.4 billion**

Source: Brookings Institution analysis of federal agency websites and FY2012 appropriations data.

a. TREAS: U.S. Department of the Treasury; HUD: U.S. Department of Housing and Urban Development; FED: Federal Reserve System; ED: U.S. Department of Education; HHS: U.S. Department of Health and Human Services; USDA: U.S. Department of Agriculture; DOT: U.S. Department of Transportation. Totals at the end of each column are in boldface.

All told, federal spending on programs that attempt to address poverty through place-based efforts amounted to $82 billion in 2012 (see table 5-1). Although this is a significant total, it looks less substantial when compared with federal spending on individual entitlement programs like the Earned Income Tax Credit ($62 billion), the Supplemental Nutrition Assistance Program (SNAP; $78 billion), or Medicaid and the State Children's Health Insurance Program ($260 billion). Moreover, that $82 billion is spread across at least ten different federal agencies and more than eighty individual programs, with little understanding as to how that spending comes together to impact poverty or increase opportunity at the community or regional level.

The Inadequacy of Current Policies in Suburbia

Nearly fifty years after the War on Poverty that launched many of these place-focused strategies, the country's collective approach is ripe for reassessment. The unparalleled magnitude and geographic reach of poverty in metropolitan America today call into question the basic theories that undergird the piecemeal, fragmented efforts to address the complex connections between poverty and place.

Moreover, as previous chapters have revealed, the "suburbia" affected by increasing poverty is not a monolith. What works in the At-Risk immigrant hubs of South King County, Washington, may not work in the Strained Suburbs of the Chicago region's middle and outer rings. At the same time, the resources that Rapid Growth communities in suburban Denver can bring to bear on rising poverty likely differ from those available in the Distressed Suburbs east of Pittsburgh.[16]

Notwithstanding the diversity of suburbia, the current system of antipoverty policies remains absent, underdeployed, or insufficiently tailored across this continuum of places. And even if the current framework could be expanded to and replicated in suburbia, should it be?

Consider efforts to *improve neighborhoods*. These strategies assume, by and large, that market failures exist at the neighborhood level, and that such neighborhoods have locational assets and advantages that render them valuable for future market activity. But that proposition does not necessarily hold across suburbs. For one, suburban poverty often spreads over much wider areas and exists in communities that lack basic infrastructure or strong connections to economic activity. This is true of Rapid Growth Suburbs like unincorporated Arapahoe County in metropolitan Denver or suburban Harris County outside of Houston. But it is also true of Distressed Suburbs like Cleveland Heights, Ohio—places that not only have aging infrastructure but also lack market value after years of decline (similar to their hardest-hit urban counterparts).

Penn Hills, a Distressed Suburb outside of Pittsburgh that was described at the beginning of chapter 4, exemplifies both ways in which neighborhood improvement strategies fail to fit suburbs. Penn Hills is an "entitlement community" for purposes of the CDBG program, meaning that the city is of sufficient size to receive funds directly from HUD for community development activities—approximately $680,000 per year in formula funding.[17] Over the 2000s, municipal officials applied varying portions of that funding toward the demolition of vacant and abandoned homes, which reflect long-term population losses occurring in the community. However, the amount of demolition Penn Hills has been able to carry out pales in comparison with the need, and local officials have little capacity for linking those efforts to broader economic and community development strategies. The city has a nascent community development corporation (CDC), but not one that is anywhere near sufficiently equipped to deal with the challenges facing its most disinvested neighborhoods.

Moreover, the structure of CDBG essentially encourages Penn Hills to try to tackle this issue on its own, rather than working collaboratively with other Allegheny County communities facing a very similar economic dynamic, perpetuating capacity challenges at the local level and failing to marshal any sort of broader vision for the region. The economic future of Distressed Suburbs like Penn Hills is hazy at best, given the myriad challenges they face and minimal resources they possess, yet federal neighborhood improvement programs do little to help clarify that future, in part because they do not operate at the scale of the issues facing struggling suburbs.

As for programs that *deliver services*, a number of factors challenge the economics of providing services and supports to needy families in suburbs. Poverty is often at once more geographically dispersed across suburbs and clustered in small, resource-strapped municipalities. Strained suburbs like outlying Fulton and Gwinnett Counties in the Atlanta region must deal with a growing poor population dispersed across large stretches of unincorporated county, just as At-Risk Suburbs like Mountlake Terrace outside of Seattle and Summit, New Jersey, near New York, must deal with significant increases in poverty in the context of a relatively small (roughly 20,000 residents) and shrinking population base. Furthermore, as described in chapter 4, delivery can be complicated by a lack of familiarity among target populations of the services available, and concerns related to stigma.

Access to subsidized primary health care provides one example of how federal service delivery programs can completely miss the growth of suburban poverty. The Consolidated Health Centers program directs competitive grants to organizations that provide health care to populations in medically underserved areas (MUAs). A bureau within the U.S. Department of Health and Human Services (HHS) designates MUAs based on data submitted by states, subject to criteria including the availability of primary care physicians, infant mortality, and the elderly and poor shares of the population. But while grantees must report annually to HHS on their activities, MUAs are updated infrequently.

In the Cleveland metropolitan area, 163 medically underserved neighborhoods in Cuyahoga and Lorain Counties were identified through 1994, based largely on data from the 1990 decennial census. At the time, those neighborhoods contained 51 percent of the metropolitan area's poor population. By the end of the 2000s, however, that share had dropped to 39 percent as poverty spread farther throughout the metropolitan area.[18] Not only are the data used to define MUAs themselves out of date, but also the neighborhood poverty rate metric itself directs services toward the *poorest* areas, not necessarily those with the *largest poor populations*. As a result, residents of suburbs with growing low-income communities on the city's western and southern borders, such as the Distressed Suburbs of Lakewood, Parma, and Berea, must travel into downtown Cleveland to access those services. Even if those federal dollars could reach the suburbs, however, it is likely that not every community in need of such services possesses the local will or capacity to provide them.

Finally, lower-income suburbs today are home to populations that have, in theory, "benefited" from policies that aimed to *expand opportunity*, particularly around housing. Yet families in many of these places still lack access to higher-quality educational and employment options, which often abound in suburbs elsewhere in the same region that have less affordable housing.

For instance, as noted earlier, the Cities of Carquinez in the Bay Area's East Contra Costa County ("East County") experienced large increases in HCV usage in the early to mid-2000s. Many participants in the program relocated to those communities from Oakland and Richmond, attracted to larger, more affordable homes in safer environs. Yet in most parts of the country, including the Bay Area, housing authorities that administer the voucher program provide little in the way of "mobility counseling" that might help renters weigh the range of community factors most important for family economic success.[19] As a result, many subsidized renters in East County suburbs ended up isolated from jobs, with limited access to public transportation, near schools that exhibit some of the same performance challenges as those in the cities they left behind, and in some cases facing a hostile community response to their arrival. Those who arrived in East County from distressed inner-city neighborhoods were likely still better off in a number of ways, but access to counseling might have connected them to superior affordable housing options elsewhere in the region. In this way, policies to expand opportunity for the inner-city poor have failed to engage the broader market forces that constrain choices and can ultimately lead to resegregation of the poor in suburbs.

Cross-Cutting Challenges to Confronting Suburban Poverty

In addition to these basic mismatches between traditional approaches and the new spatial reality of poverty and opportunity, suburbs often struggle with a host of other challenges and barriers that stand in the way of expanding and adapting any one of the three dominant strategies to meet the increasingly regional scale of need.

Lack of capacity

When it comes to the infrastructure for addressing poverty, suburbs tend to have far less public and private institutional capacity than large cities. As detailed in chapter 4, neither the uneven and overstretched nonprofit suburban safety net nor the limited philanthropic capacity in suburbia has kept up with the seismic shift in the geography of American poverty that has taken place in recent years. Moreover, suburban communities mostly lack the network of local organizations and institutions—such as CDCs—that have evolved over years of grassroots organizing and institution building in urban neighborhoods. The neighborhood improvement strategies described above are often predicated on these kinds of networks. Thus, the historical lack of organizational capacity in suburbs makes it harder for current policies and programs to respond to growing needs, given how much they depend on the presence of existing organizations and expertise.[20]

Compounding these challenges, local suburban governments often have not developed the human services and community development structures that many urban places and bigger cities have instituted over time. Even in suburbs where poverty challenges have existed for many years, local leaders often failed to build that capacity. For some this may have been a conscious decision, made in the hope that they might eventually "deflect the problem" to other communities. But for many others, the lack of capacity is indicative of the budget constraints that plague struggling suburbs and force them to make multiple tradeoffs between basic services and other needs. This is particularly true for Distressed or At-Risk Suburbs where poverty has grown while the tax base has stagnated or declined.

For instance, at a time when recession and the increased presence of renters and voucher holders required more oversight and resources, the Distressed Suburb of Lakewood, Ohio, lacked the fiscal capacity to staff its housing department to address small code enforcement issues before they grew into larger community problems. That gap is indicative of the budget pressures that strain the ability of most small jurisdictions to extend service delivery beyond core commitments like public works, public safety, and education. In contrast, Montgomery County, Maryland, has built a relatively robust safety net over the years, as illustrated in chapter 4, and has developed more capacity within county government for addressing the challenges of poverty. However, its poor population jumped by two-thirds (more than 30,000 people) after the onset of the recession, even as population growth slowed over the decade and the jobs base contracted. Amid strained resources and rapidly growing need in this At-Risk Suburb, the county has had to find ways to tap into nongovernmental capacity to respond to the needs of its increasingly diverse and low-income residents.

Extensive fragmentation and persistent silos

In part, the lack of capacity in many suburbs with growing poverty stems from jurisdictional fragmentation and, in some regions, the proliferation of decision-making bodies. These entities rarely work at the scale needed to address the challenges that accompany regionalizing poverty, and structures that encourage collaboration are patchy at best. Consider suburban Denver, where crossing County Line Road can mean losing a child care subsidy. Because neighboring Arapahoe and Douglas Counties do not coordinate on setting eligibility thresholds, following a job or housing opportunity within the same region can mean giving up critical work supports. And layering more jurisdictions onto the metropolitan map often means layering on even more challenges, as exemplified by the Chicago Southland's struggles during the foreclosure crisis. When statisticians pointed out that the foreclosure rates were actually higher in the Southland than in the city of Chicago, they were looking at an area served by forty-two different municipal governments. Not only was there no single point person, commissioner, or mayor to serve as the ultimate go-to person, but none of the forty-two towns on its own had the resources to effectively stem a crisis that spread across borders and threatened the broader region. The administrative challenges they faced in trying to map rigid government funding structures onto a collaborative approach to the crisis only underscored the barriers inherent in a fragmented system.

Furthermore, federal program silos maintained for historical, administrative purposes create inflexibility in delivery and frustrate integrated responses at the community level. They also contribute to the administrative burden of agencies or organizations delivering these services, lead to inefficiencies and redundancy, and can ultimately stifle innovation.

In Houston, Neighborhood Centers was founded more than 100 years ago as part of the settlement house movement. Today, it provides a continuum of services to low-income residents and families in more than sixty locations throughout the Houston region and across Texas—spanning inner-city neighborhoods and At-Risk and Rapid Growth Suburbs, and including programs for children, youth, seniors, and immigrants on everything from health and education to leadership and economic development, financial literacy and security, and citizenship.

To provide a seamless service experience to its participants, however, Neighborhood Centers must coordinate the distribution of resources from thirty-five different federal programs, in additional to state, local, and private sector sources. This means that it must juggle multiple, sometimes conflicting rules and regulations in areas like child nutrition, where the U.S. Department of Agriculture, HHS, and the Texas Department of Family and Protective Services all provide support. It must also file upwards of 200 different reports internally and externally on anywhere from a monthly to an annual basis, and it maintains as many as forty different computer systems to track the relevant data for those reports. The organization has a highly successful track record in serving families and communities in the Houston area despite this fragmentation, as described in the next chapter. But activities like compliance, reporting, and integration require significant investments of time and infrastructure that could be better spent pursuing core program goals.

Inefficient, inflexible, and unreliable funding

As the Chicago Southland and Neighborhood Centers examples illustrate, the current system imposes considerable constraints on providers and communities due to rigid and siloed funding structures that increase administrative burdens and hamper collaboration and innovation among recipients. Furthermore, funding for human services and community development often proves unreliable or unsustainable as government programs expire, shrink, or face uncertainty about whether they will be renewed. Likewise, philanthropic funding can provide important seed money to pilot programs or bridge funding to fill gaps in other funding sources, but foundation dollars may also prove limited over time or may be cut as foundation priorities change. The instability in the funding landscape can slow, and even corrode, efforts to build capacity in suburbia. For instance, in their research on suburban service providers, Allard and Roth found that funding reductions in 2009 led more than one in five providers (22 percent) to cut services, 13 percent to reduce case loads, and more than a quarter (28 percent) to lay off staff, even as demand for services significantly increased.[21]

For several years, the lack of adequate funding stymied the plans of Mapleton Public Schools—a suburban district outside of Denver—to bring a community health clinic onto its newest campus. The clinic was intended, first and foremost, to serve the pressing health needs of a growing low-income student population. In a decade's time, the number of students on free and reduced-price lunches in the district doubled, accounting for more than two-thirds of the student body in the 2010–11 school year. But the clinic project was also designed to serve the broader community, extending care to underserved low-income residents in the Rapid Growth Suburb of Thornton and unincorporated Adams County. Although the district worked to bring this plan to fruition for more than six years, only recently have the pieces started to fall into place.

The reliability of funding for such safety net services has only deteriorated in recent years. Federal funding for safety net and community development programs has been largely flat or declining, and continued fiscal pressures at the federal level mean that cuts to many of these agencies and programs are increasingly likely in the near future. State and local governments have already made deep cuts to close budget gaps in the wake of the Great Recession, and despite their more stable footing now, many continue to weigh additional reductions.[22] If the resources available in the current system have not been sufficient to fully meet the long-recognized challenges in urban and rural America, then that system will only find itself woefully ill equipped to meet the rapidly growing need in suburbia.

Underlying all of these issues is a lack of identified stewards to take the lead on issues of regionalizing poverty and shifting opportunity. The strained safety net, lack of organizational and fiscal capacity, and level of fragmentation in suburbia make it difficult to identify where the responsibility for action lies, which ultimately can inhibit the provision of even the most basic services. For instance, the unincorporated portion of Adams County served by Mapleton Public Schools lacks sidewalks that allow students to safely walk to school. To address this basic infrastructure issue, the school district worked with the county and galvanized support for an initiative to build a sidewalk that allows students at a nearby apartment complex to safely walk the quarter-mile to school. In the face of fragmentation and limited local capacity, juggling the needs and resources of multiple jurisdictions and engaging on simple but critical infrastructure issues was difficult at best. But as Mapleton school district superintendent Charlotte Ciancio remarked, "If not us, then who?"[23]

Conclusion

Nearly fifty years of federal policies and programs to help alleviate poverty and promote economic opportunity in lower-income places have achieved real progress. They have contributed to reductions in racial segregation and childhood hunger and to increases in affordable housing supply and quality, local commercial activity, and educational attainment.

Those policies and programs, however, have hardly eradicated the urban poverty they were largely designed to address. And now, suburban poverty poses considerable challenges to the city-oriented delivery model on which those approaches rely. The prerequisites for success—concentrated target populations; high-capacity, financially stable local government and nonprofits; market-based momentum; and the ability to orchestrate investment across dozens of siloed programs and policies—simply do not exist in most suburban communities. In fact, most inner cities lack these attributes, too.

Yet in the face of those challenges, a handful of enterprising nonprofits, collaborative organizations, and regional entities around the country are asking the same question as the suburban Denver superintendent: "If not us, then who?" They are stepping forward to confront suburban poverty and finding ways to meet the needs of the diverse array of suburbs dealing with these challenges. They, too, contend with all the barriers described above. As the Chicago Southland example at the beginning of the chapter illustrates, current policies not only fail to support smart innovation along those lines but often actively frustrate it, to the detriment of low-income families and communities in cities and suburbs alike.

Fortunately, emerging metropolitan leaders and innovators are adopting smart, tailored approaches that point the way toward a new policy framework. Notably, they share the same aims as current policies and programs—improving neighborhoods, delivering services, and expanding opportunities in low-income communities. However, they are doing those things in ways much better aligned with the reality of poverty and opportunity, and in view of the available resources, in their respective regions. The next chapter highlights several of these innovators and approaches, identifying the key tenets and best practices they share. All recognize that the legacy systems built to combat yesterday's poverty must be remade to confront the scale and geography of today's challenges.

6

Innovating Locally to Confront Suburban Poverty

Montgomery County, Maryland—a suburban county adjacent to the nation's capital—consistently ranks among the country's wealthiest counties. In 2010, it ranked twelfth in the nation for median household income at more than $89,000, well above the $50,000 national median. Within the county, communities including Bethesda, Chevy Chase, Potomac, and Rockville are home to much of the Washington region's high-paid professional class of lawyers, consultants, scientists, technology workers, and government executives.

Yet in recent years, this million-person jurisdiction has grown increasingly diverse, both demographically and economically, changing the scope and scale of need among the county's residents. The 2000s, in particular, were a period of marked transformation in Montgomery County. The early to mid-2000s brought more jobs

Montgomery County, Maryland: Apartment buildings in Wheaton, which rapidly diversified demographically and economically in the 2000s. (Jane Williams)

and people to the county and a slight drop in the number of residents living in poverty. However, the disruption of the Great Recession more than erased those gains. In just three years, Montgomery County shed more than 37,000 jobs, dropping below its 2000 jobs total by 2010. At the same time, the number of residents living below the federal poverty line grew by two-thirds, or more than 30,000 people, pushing the poverty rate up by nearly 3 percentage points between 2007 and 2010. No other county in the Washington region, including the District of Columbia, experienced increases in poverty of this magnitude during the 2000s.

The 2000s also marked a period of growing ethnic and racial diversity in Montgomery County. Indeed, the 2010 census revealed that, for the first time, non-Hispanic whites constituted less than half (49 percent) of the county's residents, down from 73 percent two decades earlier. Whereas immigrants accounted for fewer than one in five residents in 1990, in 2010 they represented almost one-third of the population and almost 40 percent of poor residents.

As chronicled in the previous chapters, such rapid increases in poverty, coupled with the shifting demographic makeup of the community, often leave community leaders playing catch-up without the resources to match. Yet Montgomery County officials and service providers recognized the changing needs of a diversifying population and anticipated the growing demands that would arise as the Great Recession began to take hold. In 2006, the newly elected county executive, Isiah (Ike) Leggett, signaled that the county recognized the transitions under way and the need to leverage resources beyond what it alone could provide. The county established an Office of Community Partnerships (OCP), with the mission to "strengthen relationships between the Montgomery County government and the residents it serves, with special focus on underserved and emerging communities and our neighbors in need."[1]

In 2009, during the deepest part of the recession, officials from OCP and the county's Department of Health and Human Services came together with the support of the Community Foundation of Montgomery County to partner with leaders from the faith-based community, social service nonprofits, and grassroots organizations led by IMPACT Silver Spring to develop strategies for making sure diverse communities in need did not miss out on critical emergency and safety net services because of lack of information or cultural barriers. This partnership launched the Neighborhood Opportunity Network, a cross-sector collaboration that seeks to ensure that emergency services (county or nonprofit) reach residents in need, and to create community connections and networks in suburbs where such resources are lacking. The initiative uses door-knocking campaigns to identify needs and alert residents to services available at newly created Neighborhood Service Centers. These centers are staffed by "Community Connectors" who guide residents through various application processes. The network also promotes participatory community sessions and small meetings of neighbors to build relationships, identify issues and needs, and share resources. As OCP director Bruce Adams writes, the Neighborhood Opportunity Network model "has replaced the traditional charity/social services approach to emergency service delivery with a culturally competent capacity building model."[2]

In many ways, the proactive and collaborative approach that emerged in Montgomery County mirrors the actions of innovators in metropolitan areas across the country who have developed strategies that address the growing scale of need in more efficient and effective ways. Discussions, site visits, and meetings with a diverse group of these innovators point to three tenets that characterize their models for overcoming the barriers highlighted in the previous chapter:

—*Achieving scale*, either through their geographic service area or through the range of services and functions they provide;

—*Collaborating* to overcome jurisdictional and programmatic fragmentation and to bridge public and private sectors; and

—*Funding strategically*, by creatively using government and philanthropic support and pursuing market-oriented vehicles to leverage private investment.

The organizations and approaches we highlight in this chapter bring these elements together in different ways to address various aspects of the changing geography of poverty and opportunity. To provide a view of the broad scope of scaled, collaborative, and enterprising work going on in regions across the country, we explore each tenet in turn below.

Achieving Scale

As detailed in chapter 5, current place-based policy responses to poverty are fragmented in two key ways that produce misalignment with the realities of contemporary suburban needs. First, they divide the range of services needed to strengthen whole families and communities into a series of narrow, differently structured programs that frustrate coordination. Second, they support interventions confined largely to the local or neighborhood level that fail to recognize the increasingly metropolitan nature of poverty.

However, organizations like Houston's Neighborhood Centers have evolved to a scale that tackles both types of fragmentation challenges. Neighborhood Centers has an annual budget of approximately $275 million that draws on dozens of federal, state, and private funding sources to deliver a range of services in both urban and suburban communities. In doing so, the organization manages to serve its clients in a largely seamless fashion, in part owing to its scale, which provides numerous advantages:

—The size of Neighborhood Centers gives it the means to invest in critical infrastructure, including up-to-date information technology and high-grade facilities, which in turn increase both its administrative efficiency and the quality of the services it provides. For instance, it can use information captured through its income tax assistance program for lower-income workers and families to understand neighborhood income dynamics and target other services where they are most needed. Its size also allows it to offer salaries that are more competitive with those in the private sector, so the organization can attract top management talent and increase its operational capacity.

—Neighborhood Centers benefits from a stable base of public sector funding, with much of it coming from multiyear contracts for administering programs under Head Start and the Workforce Investment Act. Access to that stable base enables the organization to make strategic expenditures on "venture" activities that address emerging community needs and over time can increase the breadth and effectiveness of its services. For instance, Neighborhood Centers' acquisition of a smaller nonprofit focused on senior services gave it the opportunity to conduct an assessment of senior needs in the community, which led to the development of a broader "aging in place" program.

—Although government funding makes up a significant portion of Neighborhood Centers' revenues, its activities draw on a wide range of contracts, agencies, and private sector backers that help mitigate the risk associated with any one source of funding. Its large-scale community centers, such as Cleveland-Ripley Neighborhood Center in the Houston suburb of Pasadena, draw on a balanced mix of public, private, and earned revenue. The track record of Neighborhood Centers in maintaining these diverse sources also serves as a marker of performance that has bolstered funder confidence.

—The presence of Neighborhood Centers in so many corners of the Houston metropolitan area also enables it to respond rapidly and comprehensively to regional crises and opportunities. Within days of Hurricane

Katrina making landfall in 2005, Neighborhood Centers created the Stay Connected Initiative to meet the longer-term needs of the tens of thousands of evacuees who would eventually settle in the Houston region. When Hurricane Ike hit in 2008, the organization was thus positioned as the provider of first choice for administering social services and housing assistance.

To scale successfully, Neighborhood Centers has made significant investments in its administrative capacity, committing staff and resources to the active maintenance of contracts and grants and to the evaluation of program data and outcomes. At the same time, its effectiveness also derives from the ways in which it marries scale with a customized service model. Neighborhood Centers streamlines what can be standardized and made more efficient, while investing the time and money to engage community residents, business owners, elected officials, service providers, and others to understand the strengths and assets of each community it serves, tailoring its response accordingly.

This approach is evident in the Cleveland-Ripley Neighborhood Center located in the At-Risk Suburb of Pasadena described in chapter 4. The center serves a community that has undergone significant demographic change during the past few decades as it shifted from a community of largely middle-class white families to a more diverse place with a growing segment of lower-middle-class Hispanic residents. Amid these changes, Neighborhood Centers found that the community's vision for its future included gaining greater access to and influence on local institutions for its Hispanic members, securing adequate public transportation (there was none in Pasadena at the time), and increasing opportunities for adult education. By 2013, thanks to a strong strategic alliance with the Harris County Department of Education, the Cleveland-Ripley center was the largest ESL (English as a second language) and adult education center for both Pasadena and Neighborhood Centers, with more than 1,000 students enrolled annually. To address transportation needs, the Cleveland-Ripley community advisory board sparked a partnership between Harris County and the cities of Pasadena and neighboring La Porte, which led to the creation of a public bus line that connects these two communities to each other and to Houston public transit. Cleveland-Ripley staff and volunteers made gains toward increasing the recognition of Latino residents in the community by taking the lead in forming the Census Count Committee for Pasadena in the spring of 2009. The committee succeeded in significantly boosting local participation in the 2010 Census and paving the way toward greater representation for Hispanics.

As a high-capacity regional human services provider, Neighborhood Centers represents one model for overcoming the fragmentation that often stymies effective responses to the shifting geography of poverty and opportunity. In other parts of the country, leadership has emerged from different sectors and at different levels of geography to adopt a more systemic approach to integrating services.

States, in particular, can help facilitate program access for families in areas of new or increasing poverty. Along those lines, the Urban Institute, with assistance from the Center on Budget and Policy Priorities, launched the Work Support Strategies: Streamlining Access, Strengthening Families initiative.[3] The initiative helps a selected group of states design, test, and implement more integrated, streamlined, and efficient systems that improve access to key work supports for low-income families. In North Carolina, a state whose work support programs are county administered and state supervised, the Department of Health and Human Services' pilot project is working to "build on the rollout of NC-FAST, an integrated, automated system for eligibility determination" to cut county workloads, improve service delivery, and speed application review, so that families need only "'tell their story once' and get everything they need."[4] Such improvements stand to benefit low-income suburban families, who often face greater geographic and informational barriers to accessing the array of supports for which they qualify.

Getting to scale is also a key preoccupation among innovative community development financial institutions (CDFIs). CDFIs serve communities that lack access to credit and consumer financial services. To be certified as a CDFI by the U.S. Treasury Department (and thus to be eligible for related public and private investment programs), an organization must demonstrate that at least 65 percent of its total lending, services, and other activities benefit low-income communities. Today, a growing number of CDFIs are leveraging their community development knowledge, technical expertise, and financing to expand their efforts far beyond the distressed urban and rural neighborhoods in which they originated.

Some CDFIs are working at a multistate or national level to scale their geographic footprint and service model. IFF (formerly the Illinois Facilities Fund) was launched in 1988 as a loan fund for the capital needs of Illinois nonprofits serving low-income and special needs populations. Over the years, IFF has grown to serve five states in the Midwest—Illinois, Indiana, Iowa, Missouri, and Wisconsin—and has expanded its portfolio of services to include real estate consulting and development as well as research and public policy activities. IFF's in-house capacity has enabled it to identify and respond to the shifting geography of need across its expanding service area. For instance, in 2003 IFF released an analysis of gaps in the supply of subsidized early childhood care and education services relative to the eligible population in Illinois counties and major municipalities. Based on its findings, IFF secured funding from the Grand Victoria Foundation to support the financing and development or expansion of early childhood care and education capacity in eleven underserved Chicago suburbs with growing low-income populations. In 2004, IFF added a housing division, primarily to serve suburban communities that lacked consistently operating, locally based community development corporations or affordable housing developers.

Other CDFIs are using a franchise model to expand their national and metropolitan footprints. The Milwaukee-based CDFI Ways to Work helps low-income families with challenging credit histories obtain reliable transportation to get to work, a particularly relevant service for the suburban poor, who often live in communities with limited or no public transit options. Ways to Work finances affordable auto loans for these families through a blend of public and private dollars, and contracts with partner agencies to provide wraparound financial capacity building services to program participants. Ways to Work has scaled this approach geographically by locating loan offices in agencies that belong to its sister organization's network (Alliance for Children and Families), building on existing provider capacity and client relationships. Through this franchise approach, Ways to Work has extended its program to urban, suburban, and rural communities in more than fifty sites in twenty-one states.

In a world of large-scale problems and limited resources, size matters. Small organizations and narrow programs are a fundamental mismatch for the increasingly metropolitan reach of poverty. Scaled solutions such as those profiled here have the potential to bring efficiency, expertise, and entrepreneurialism to the challenges facing low-income people and communities in cities and suburbs alike.

Collaborating

Of course, not every suburban community has a Neighborhood Centers or an IFF at its doorstep. Many are not located in large counties like Montgomery County that possess the organizational and fiscal capacity to act at scale. Where scaled individual solutions are not within reach, enterprising governments and nonprofits are increasingly collaborating to overcome the fragmentation and proliferation of systems, sectors, jurisdictions, and agencies.

In the Chicago region multiple municipal collaborative entities have emerged in the suburbs since the late 2000s, ringing the city from north to south, each focused on the revitalization and inclusive development of older suburban communities.[5] Notwithstanding the challenges it initially faced in connecting to federal foreclosure assistance dollars, the Chicago Southland Housing and Community Development Collaborative (CSHCDC) has grown in both capacity and resources, hiring a full-time coordinator in 2009 with primary support from the Chicago Community Trust and the Grand Victoria Foundation. The coordinator, housed within the South Suburban Mayors and Managers Association, helps connect the collaborative to regional, state, and federal resources and takes the lead on crafting applications for public and private funding.

Today, the collaborative consists of twenty-three Chicago Southland municipalities and has secured almost $25 million for housing and community development through various government sources, including the Neighborhood Stabilization Program (NSP), the federal Community Development Block Grant (CDBG) Disaster Recovery Program, and the Sustainable Communities Initiative. With those funds, CSHCDC has begun to rehabilitate and demolish foreclosed and blighted properties, launched a Transit-Oriented Development (TOD) Fund, founded a land bank to facilitate the acquisition and repurposing of vacant and blighted properties, and created a GIS (geographic information system) mapping system to track demographic and economic trends and help neighboring towns prioritize a joint development pipeline to efficiently and transparently target investments.

Another collaborative that emerged alongside CSHCDC comprises five communities in Chicago's western suburbs—Bellwood, Berwyn, Forest Park, Maywood, and Oak Park. At the height of the housing crisis, their collective foreclosure rate outstripped the regional average, prompting these communities to launch their own interjurisdictional collaboration to apply jointly for first-round NSP funds.[6] Like the CSHCDC, the West Cook County Housing Collaborative (WCCHC) came together with technical assistance and support from regional intermediaries, including the Metropolitan Mayors Caucus, the Metropolitan Planning Council (MPC), and the Chicago Metropolitan Agency for Planning (CMAP), and received primary support from the Chicago Community Trust and the Grand Victoria Foundation to hire a coordinator. However, rather than selecting an individual who would be housed in the local council of governments, WCCHC engaged IFF to act in that role, drawing on the CDFI's in-house capacity and experience as a developer. The collaborative has attracted over $10 million in NSP, CDBG Disaster Recovery, and Sustainable Communities Initiative funds. Those investments have funded the rehabilitation of rental housing and foreclosed single-family homes, helped launch a TOD Fund, improved GIS and housing prioritization tools, and leveraged employer-assisted housing outreach and engagement.

Both collaboratives benefited from a series of factors that helped them coalesce and move these projects forward. For instance, the Metropolitan Mayors Caucus, a regionwide association of 272 mayors first convened in 1997, had provided support and leadership to the forerunners of these collaboratives in the late 1990s and early 2000s. MPC connected the collaboratives to regional, state, and federal resources and best practices. With support from CMAP, the area's metropolitan planning organization, these partners guided the creation and implementation of comprehensive development plans in each cluster. Financial support from the Chicago Community Trust, later buoyed by grants from other local foundations like the Grand Victoria Foundation and Field Foundation, funded the staffing and capacity necessary to formalize and strengthen the collaborative structures.

Collaboration also paved the way for tackling the issues facing these communities in a much more comprehensive and ultimately effective way. Grounded in analysis of projected changes in community demographics and housing needs, the collaboratives' plans link housing with transportation and economic development to prioritize TOD and create a shared vision for how to pursue development across the collaborative as a whole. Leaders within each collaborative agreed to approach these issues on a larger scale, even if funds awarded or redevelopment undertaken did not directly target their municipality. They have also realized administrative cost savings and increased impact resulting from their coordinated approach.

Truly regional responses to the range of issues affecting low-income people and communities remain rare. But these collaborative models in the Chicago region show how groups of jurisdictions that first came together to address the housing crisis have built on that momentum to pursue broader community economic development goals. These efforts have an increasing number of analogues in regions across the country.

Some approaches cut across issue areas and alter the geographic governance of service delivery. The state of Ohio recently launched an effort to directly address the challenges that arise from severe jurisdictional fragmentation in many of its regions, particularly as needs have grown and tax revenues have taken a hit during a down economy. The Local Government Innovation Fund (LGIF), adopted in 2011, provides a combination of grants and loans to local governments to study or implement shared services, collaborative demonstration projects, and mergers among jurisdictions. These strategies are meant to help ameliorate the effects of deep budget cuts at the local level in recent years, by improving service delivery to residents while reducing the costs of providing services across jurisdictions. A number of Cleveland suburbs, including Moreland Hills, Orange, Pepper Pike, and Woodmere on the city's east side, were among the first pool of recipients to receive LGIF funds to study merger and shared-service models.

Other approaches unite jurisdictions around critical single-issue areas such as education. In 2010, a consortium of public, private, and nonprofit stakeholders in the Seattle region launched the Road Map Project. The project, coordinated by the Center for Community Education Results, aims to double postsecondary attainment and close achievement gaps for low-income and minority students in six school districts in King County's southern suburbs (Auburn, Federal Way, Highline, Kent, Renton, and Tukwila) and public schools in South Seattle. Of the students in the seven districts who speak 167 different primary languages, 58 percent receive free and reduced-price lunches (versus 42 percent regionwide) and 66 percent are students of color (versus 42 percent regionwide).[7]

Through the Road Map Project, the seven districts are working together on a series of initiatives that embrace a "cradle to college/career" approach to improve educational outcomes. Work groups with representation from the participating districts and other regional stakeholders meet regularly to review the latest performance data, develop strategies, and implement action plans to address the needs of different groups, including young children from birth to third grade, English language learners, and those making the transition to postsecondary education. They have adopted a common set of metrics to track progress toward a goal of doubling the number of students in the Road Map region who are on track to graduate or earn a career credential by 2020. In this respect, Seattle is a leader among a growing number of regions employing similar collaborative approaches that build on the Strive Partnership model conceived in Greater Cincinnati in 2006.[8] The U.S. Department of Education recognized the Road Map Project's leadership in December 2012 with a $40 million Race to the Top grant focused on personalizing education across the Road Map region and helping more children prepare for success in postsecondary education, particularly in the STEM (science, technology, engineering, and mathematics) fields that characterize jobs in Seattle's regional economy.[9]

Metropolitan-level planning has also given rise to a number of initiatives that cut across both sectors and jurisdictions to contend with the new scale of need and opportunity. In the San Francisco Bay Area, for instance, the Transit-Oriented Affordable Housing (TOAH) Fund—a collaboration led by the Great Communities Collaborative, the Association of Bay Area Governments, and the Metropolitan Transportation Commission—provides financing for affordable housing, retail space, and services like child care centers, fresh food outlets, and health clinics near transit lines throughout nine counties in the Bay Area. A number of national and regional CDFIs act as originating lenders, including the Corporation for Supportive Housing, the Enterprise Community Loan Fund, the Local Initiatives Support Corporation (LISC), the Northern California Community Loan Fund, and the Low Income Investment Fund (LIIF, which also acts as fund manager). To be eligible for financing, projects must be located in a Priority Development Area (PDA). More than sixty jurisdictions, both cities and suburbs throughout the region, have identified PDAs, which are areas that provide opportunities for infill development (that is, development of vacant or underused properties in existing communities).[10]

Social services are another area in which coordination among multiple suburban municipalities is improving planning and service delivery in some regions. The South King Council of Human Services is an umbrella organization that supports research and information sharing, provides technical assistance, and conducts policy advocacy for social service providers across several jurisdictions in Seattle's south suburbs. Outside of Atlanta, the Gwinnett Coalition for Health and Human Services serves a similar function in what until recently was a white, middle-class county, but which has seen rising poverty during the past two decades.[11]

In an American governance system characterized by local control, suburban jurisdictions are accustomed to competing with one another for wealthy residents, new infrastructure, and commercial development. Yet as more suburbs confront the reality of growing poverty and the need to connect their residents to economic opportunity, collaboration—across places and across sectors—is slowly taking root. It remains the exception rather than the norm but signals another promising way that smaller, fragmented actors are finding scale in the absence of high-capacity delivery systems.

Funding Strategically

Siloed, inflexible, and insufficient funding streams compound the problems of fragmentation and hamper efforts to alleviate poverty and promote opportunity in suburbia. Against the backdrop of the outdated and often unwieldy system for addressing poverty in place, leaders across the country have crafted strategic and innovative funding models to mitigate these shortcomings as they address rapidly rising and geographically shifting need.

In fact, the foundation of many of the examples described above— from Neighborhood Centers to the collaboratives in Chicago's suburbs to the Bay Area's TOAH Fund—is a diversified funding model that blends public and private dollars to increase efficiencies and impact. In many ways, the ability to strategically leverage multiple revenue sources is a requirement for any high-performing institution in today's fiscal and political landscape.

In the face of strained and dwindling resources, new vehicles and pioneering models are emerging that stretch limited resources and sharpen the focus on outcomes. The Mortgage Resolution Fund (MRF) is one example. As the foreclosure crisis worsened, four national organizations—Enterprise Community Partners, Housing Partnership Network, Mercy Portfolio Services (a subsidiary of Mercy Housing), and the National Community Stabilization Trust—collaborated in 2011 to develop a strategy that would address gaps in the existing approaches to the crisis. In their view, the challenges were threefold. First, NSP funds provided an important federal resource for dealing with foreclosure-affected communities but were not sufficient to meet growing needs. Second, HUD-supported foreclosure counseling agencies frequently encountered barriers in their efforts to negotiate principal reductions with overwhelmed large mortgage servicers. And third, private capital lacked sufficient incentives to work in distressed markets where expenses are higher and foreclosure processes are lengthy.

To address these challenges, these four organizations developed a joint approach that intervened earlier in the process, with a focus on keeping homeowners in their homes. They created MRF as a vehicle through which they could identify and acquire nonperforming loans, help homeowners avoid foreclosure, and reduce instances of vacant and blighted properties, which can further destabilize neighborhood home values. MRF provides a continuum of services: purchasing nonperforming loans from servicers and banks at a discount; modifying mortgages (primarily through principal reductions) based on current market values and the borrower's ability to pay; providing education and debt management support to borrowers to help them stay in their homes; and recapitalizing mortgages.

The innovative financing model behind MRF's approach was enabled by the U.S. Treasury Department's Hardest Hit Fund, established in February 2010 to assist states that had suffered the worst effects of the foreclosure crisis.[12] Using those funds, in 2011 MRF negotiated a zero-interest, long-term, no-recourse loan of $100 million from the Illinois Housing Development Authority. To date, MRF has used that financing to purchase 270 nonperforming mortgages, mostly concentrated in four suburban clusters in the Chicago region that have been disproportionately affected by the foreclosure crisis.[13]

Deploying federal place-based funds in this way is novel and strategic in a few key respects. First, the funds supported a collaborative of organizations that brought complementary skill sets and capacities to the table, helping to leverage expertise and balance responsibilities across the four institutions and their private sector partners:

—**Enterprise Community Partners** takes responsibility for fund management and compliance reporting, as well as audit and treasury functions (that is, managing the movement of funds).

—The **Housing Partnership Network** manages all mortgage resolution specialist activities and provides homeowners with education, budgeting, debt management, and decision-making support.

—**Mercy Portfolio Services**, MRF's managing member, oversees all service contracts with private sector partners (for example, for mortgage due diligence and valuation as well as transferring and servicing loans), engages the capital markets to acquire mortgages, provides back-office support (for example, accounting, human resources, information technology, and Hardest Hit Fund compliance reporting), evaluates distressed notes, and makes investment recommendations.

—The **National Community Stabilization Trust** educates its servicer network of banks, government-sponsored entities (for example, Fannie Mae), the Federal Housing Administration, and government agencies about MRF and enlists their assistance in locating and acquiring nonperforming loans within their portfolios.

Second, rather than providing *program* funding to support specific actions and interventions, the Hardest Hit funds are invested at the *enterprise* level in MRF. In Illinois, MRF negotiated a no-interest, no-recourse loan from the government that will be repaid based on MRF's ability to purchase and restructure mortgages in the private market. This enterprise-level investment allows for a flexible application of funds focused on outcomes, not outputs. For instance, in addition to focusing on the status of the mortgage, MRF's multipronged approach also provides wraparound services to borrowers. Those services not only increase the likelihood that the restructured loans will succeed; they also provide broader benefits to the community by reducing the number of foreclosures and vacant and blighted properties—meeting public policy goals through a market-oriented approach.

Other innovators nationwide are developing initiatives grounded in the same principles as the MRF example—market-oriented, enterprise-level, outcome-focused models that leverage public and private dollars to address gaps and barriers in funding for poverty alleviation efforts. A handful of philanthropies have embraced enterprise-level investment to expand capacity and find new ways of fulfilling their mission. For instance, Venture Philanthropy Partners (VPP) is a philanthropic investment organization serving the National Capital Region around Washington, D.C. VPP applies a venture philanthropy model to social service funding, with the goal of increasing the capacity and impact of high-performing leaders and organizations working to improve the lives and opportunities of low-income children. VPP concentrates its investments and technical assistance on high-capacity organizations to help institutions get to scale. In the years following the Great Recession, it helped five established District of Columbia–based nonprofits expand their services into underserved Maryland suburbs, building capacity in communities that had experienced a rapid increase in low-income residents.

Other innovators are identifying new, market-based sources of revenue to alleviate the problems facing low-income and economically distressed urban and suburban communities. The nonprofit Cuyahoga Land Bank in the Cleveland metropolitan area strategically acquires vacant and foreclosed properties in municipalities throughout the county, with the goal of returning them to productive use through rehabilitation, sale to new owners, demolition, or creative reuse (for example, gardens, green spaces, storm water management). Each municipality acts as a partner in deciding how properties will be handled, and because the land bank operates at the county scale, communities are able to spread risk and ease joint code enforcement. The primary funding for Cuyahoga Land Bank comes from penalties and interest on delinquent real estate taxes and assessments. Supplemental funds come from the land bank's partners, the sale of land bank properties to qualified developers, as well as donations and the recoupment of funds from banks. This approach has been expanded throughout northern Ohio through the Thriving Communities Institute, which is setting up a network of county land banks operating on a similar model.

Another emerging model is social impact investing, or the leveraging of private dollars to fund social services.[14] Social Impact Bonds (SIBs), which are also sometimes referred to as "Pay for Success" contracts, are one example. These vehicles raise private investment capital to fund prevention and early intervention services that improve social outcomes and reduce costs to government over the long term. Private investors absorb the up-front risk and invest in social service nonprofits. The government only repays investors if promised outcomes are achieved, as determined by an outside evaluator. SIBs and Pay for Success contracts are not a viable pathway to funding core safety net services, but they offer possible ways to fund targeted interventions with measurable outcomes.

Such models are relatively new and have yet to be evaluated, although some communities and levels of government are testing them. Great Britain launched the first SIB pilot in September 2010, when Social Finance UK used SIBs to finance a prisoner rehabilitation program in Peterborough. In the United States, the U.S. Department of Labor is the first federal agency to pilot this approach through its Pay for Success pilot projects. Its Workforce Innovation Fund will provide $20 million to projects that address difficult workforce issues, such as barriers to employment for hard-to-employ populations, including the homeless, former prisoners, and high school dropouts. To qualify for the pilot program, projects require several participants: a state or local agency to act as the grant applicant; an intermediary to take responsibility for achieving outcomes, contracting with providers, and engaging investors; investors to provide the up-front capital; and an outside evaluator to monitor and assess results.

A handful of states also are moving forward with Pay for Success pilots. Minnesota's 2011 Pay for Performance Act authorized a Human Capital Performance Bond (HUCAP) pilot. Similar to SIBs, HUCAP bonds are state annual appropriation bonds—purchased by private investors and financial institutions expecting market-rate returns—that will fund high-performing human service organizations, likely in the workforce development and supportive housing arena. Massachusetts also announced two Pay for Success pilots in 2012 as part of its Social Innovation Financing program. One pilot addresses chronic homelessness, and the other focuses on reducing recidivism for young men leaving the juvenile justice system. Massachusetts selected Third Sector Capital Partners, a nonprofit financial advisory firm based in Cambridge, Massachusetts, to develop and raise capital for both pilots. Third Sector Capital Partners is also working with Cuyahoga County to develop a Pay for Success pilot with the goals of improving county services, lowering taxes, increasing government efficiency, and accelerating innovation around interventions that address the challenges of target populations (for example, child welfare and youth mental and behavioral health services). Finally, with financing from Goldman Sachs and philanthropic support from the Bloomberg Foundation, the city of New York launched an SIB in 2012 targeted at reducing recidivism among young adults on Rikers Island.

The Importance of Intermediaries

Whether scaled, collaborative, or financially enterprising (or all three), many of the solutions described here benefit from, or rely on, intermediaries. These are not intermediaries in the sense of simple fiscal agents funneling resources between different actors, but scaled entities working to untangle and navigate the convoluted map of current services and funding streams to develop innovative, effective, and more efficient solutions across geographies.

These innovations use different types of organizations in the intermediary role. In many of these models, CDFIs—like Enterprise Community Partners, IFF, LIIF, and LISC—play key roles, using in-house capacity as lenders, developers, researchers, or policy advocates to shape community development across metropolitan regions. In other instances, organizations with a regional or subregional footprint, such as Chicago's MPC, the Bay Area's Great Communities Collaborative, or the Seattle region's Road Map Project, help localities connect to resources, best practices, technical assistance, and planning support. Intermediaries also increasingly provide the capacity and expertise to sift, aggregate, track, and evaluate data on the shifting dynamics that affect need and access to opportunity. Moreover, intermediaries—whether CDFIs, collaborative entities, or nonprofits—are often positioned to provide a regional context for planning and decisionmaking on issues that cross borders and intersect with an array of policy areas from education to hunger, housing, transportation, employment opportunities, and work supports.

Conclusion

We identify the examples described in this chapter as "innovations" for a reason. They are pathbreaking responses to the new realities associated with confronting poverty and promoting opportunity at the regional scale. Leaders in different sectors and from the national to the local level are finding ways to work within and around the constraints of the current antipoverty policy framework to address the complex challenges that accompany regionalizing poverty.

However, these approaches are not the norm in antipoverty practice today. Public policies and private capacities have not caught up to the fast-moving trends that have upended the traditional relationships between poverty and place in metropolitan areas. Indeed, antiquated thinking and rules have complicated the ability of these innovations to take root. The next chapter describes new approaches that will be needed to bring about the scale, collaboration, and strategic funding upon which successful efforts will depend in the era of suburban poverty.

CHAPTER **7**

Modernizing the Metropolitan Opportunity Agenda

In November 2011, a group of representatives from local organizations met in Bay Point, California, one of the Cities of Carquinez at the eastern edge of the San Francisco Bay Area. All of the participants, who included professionals in workforce development, homelessness and hunger prevention, legal aid, human services, philanthropy, and community organizing, were involved in the effort to help area families and communities contend with rising poverty and need in the wake of a devastating recession.

After they shared stories of the rapid changes that coursed through East Contra Costa County ("East County") before and after the housing market crash, and noted the unprecedented demands their organizations were facing, a representative from a local faith-based coalition related that members of more than ten congregations had come together for an "action" on a recent Saturday. When asked what issue they had focused on, he replied: "Jobs, immigration, health care, housing, schools, public safety." In other words, just about everything.

Although everyone was concerned about the numerous issues facing the community, no one seemed to have the capacity to act. Local service providers were thinly staffed and underresourced. Contra Costa County was making significant cuts in services to close a yawning budget gap. Most private philanthropy remained rooted in core cities, such as Oakland and Richmond, or in the neighborhoods of major employers in other suburbs, such as Dublin and Pleasanton. Local Contra Costa media that might have publicized these issues in the past had reduced their coverage because of budget cuts.

The Cities of Carquinez were, in a way, suffering an identity crisis. The suburbanization of poverty had transformed them but left them in a policy blind spot. Most local municipal officials had come into office during the housing boom and represented the interests of developers and the middle class, not the diverse populations suffering most from the crash. The "mental map" of poverty among state policymakers in Sacramento had not caught up with the new reality, leaving local providers at a disadvantage in the scramble for scarce state dollars. Federal stimulus programs to prevent homelessness found their way to seasoned organizations in the western part of the county, not to their eastern counterparts. However, efforts to bring experienced providers into East County faced resistance from local stakeholders who opposed "outside" solutions.

Meanwhile, the Bay Area as a whole faced serious questions about the future of these communities. East County was too big and too complicated to survive as just a bedroom suburb for the core of the region. It needed real economic development, more comprehensive local services, an affordable housing strategy, and better connections to the rest of the region. But new climate change laws in California were placing pressure on regions to reduce carbon emissions, and Bay Area planners worried that further investing in the auto-dependent, far-flung East County communities could put many more cars on the highway and cut against those new environmental imperatives.

The members and leaders of local East County organizations cared deeply about and understood their communities, no less than their counterparts in any inner-city neighborhood. They knew that the history of these places—former industrial cities with diverse populations and economies—was richer and more complex than the recent boom and bust indicated. These organizations were taking smart steps, like collaborating across issue areas (for example, housing, workforce, financial stability) where they could serve whole families more effectively.[1] But they were overwhelmed by the challenges, and they lacked a supportive policy framework that could help them confront those challenges at scale and also might have prevented them in the first place.

As the previous chapters have illuminated, many suburban communities could tell a tale similar to that of the Cities of Carquinez. The details might differ, but the sense of identity crisis and an inadequate policy architecture would persist.

Fortunately, the innovative responses bubbling up from around the country point the way toward a new framework for confronting suburban poverty. Indeed, these places and their populations do not need a "suburban solution" so much as a smarter vision to promote opportunity for their families and communities regardless of geography.

The Current Fiscal and Political Environment

Local innovations suggest the outlines of a new system for addressing the modern map of metropolitan poverty and opportunity. But what resources exist to support that system?

As chapter 5 described, investment in the current urban-oriented framework remains relatively modest and has failed to keep up with the growing and geographically expanding need of the past decade. At the same time, other parts of the safety net that have grown in response to the economic downturn—including programs with stimulative effects for local economies, like the Earned Income Tax Credit (EITC), the Supplementary Nutritional Assistance Program (SNAP, formerly known as food stamps), and extended unemployment insurance—did so largely through temporary measures. In fact, looming cuts at the federal level and continued budgetary strain among states and localities mean that, by necessity, a remade system must be designed effectively to do more with less.

At the federal level, government spending is likely to change in significant ways in the coming years. The combination of a deep recession, slow growth, and the aftereffects of tax cuts and increased military spending in the 2000s left the federal debt at 73 percent of gross domestic product (GDP) by the end of 2012—the highest level since 1950.[2] Meanwhile, the aging of the baby-boom generation is placing new pressures on health care spending in Medicare and Medicaid. Two high-profile fiscal commissions convened in 2010 and 2011 concluded that, alongside modest revenue increases, entitlements and domestic discretionary spending should be downsized significantly to bring the budget back into balance.[3] Under any scenario, tenuous current funding for the safety net could suffer further.

Yet cutbacks at the federal level do not represent the only constraints to funding an antipoverty, pro-opportunity agenda. As Ellen Seidman observed:

> The challenges at the federal level are replicated and amplified at the state and local levels, where both funds specifically targeted to lower-income communities and monies to support broader infrastructure development, upkeep, and basic services (such as police, fire, and schools) have been hard hit by a stagnant economy, reduced property values and property tax revenues, and reduced transfers from the federal and state government, at a time when the demand for services is increasing.[4]

Indeed, a National League of Cities survey found that even in 2012, three years after the recession ended, most local governments were still dealing with the aftereffects of the downturn. Of the cities surveyed, 48 percent reported reducing the size of their workforce in 2012, one-third delayed or canceled infrastructure projects, 21 percent cut spending on human services, and 19 percent cut education funding.[5] In short, creating a more scaled, more efficient, and more flexible system that can adapt to the regionalizing nature of poverty is not only good policy but is necessary in light of the limited scope for increased government spending in the years to come.

One place to start is to establish what government *must* do to provide lower-income families and communities with a platform for success, no matter where they live. Highly effective and administratively efficient federal programs such as the EITC, the Child Tax Credit, SNAP, and subsidized health insurance (through new tax credits, Medicaid, and the Children's Health Insurance Program) help families, especially those with children, meet their basic needs. To borrow President Clinton's phrase, they ensure that those who "work hard and play by the rules" are not poor.[6] Only the federal government possesses the scale and reach to establish this platform, without which more targeted strategies would remain woefully insufficient.

Beyond those baseline responsibilities, efficiencies and savings in addressing poverty and opportunity can be gained at all levels of the system—whether through reforms in current programs, or by promoting efficiency through public and private sector innovation.

The remainder of this chapter lays out a series of principles and recommendations—for federal, state, and local government as well as private sector leaders—for a smarter framework for alleviating poverty and promoting access to opportunity. We draw on lessons learned from the innovative examples highlighted in the previous chapter and suggest both practical short-term reforms and larger overhauls for the long term.

Getting to Scale

Small-bore, neighborhood-defined approaches to poverty alleviation were one of the hallmarks of the War on Poverty. Those place-based efforts have had a mixed track record, but even the most successful of those policies, and the organizations they spawned, are not fit to form for the current moment. And while the evolution of the community development field offers lessons for future efforts, recreating community development for the suburbs is neither feasible nor appropriate to the scale of the problem.

In the absence of additional resources, in order to help places throughout metropolitan areas meet the new challenges of improving low-income residents' access to opportunity, public policy must value and prioritize scale. Scaled approaches offer the promise of delivering better outcomes with the same, or even fewer, inputs. As Urban Institute president Sarah Wartell put it, "instead of scaling back, we need to figure out how to get $1.20 of value from $0.80."[7] That is a tall order, but policymakers, funders, and service providers can pave the way for scaled solutions in the near term by focusing on actionable reforms that:

—improve systems and networks,

—promote high-performance organizations, and

—support smart consolidation.

Efforts to *improve systems and networks* must begin at the federal level, where much of the programmatic fragmentation and red tape originates. Consider the experiences of Neighborhood Centers detailed in previous chapters. This organization operates programs that draw on roughly thirty-five different federal funding sources housed in eight different federal agencies. Many of these funds do not flow directly to Neighborhood Centers but instead pass through a variety of state and local governments and other intermediaries (for example, the city of Houston, regional Workforce Investment Boards, the state of Texas Health and Human Services Commission).

Neighborhood Centers weaves these federal dollars with other state, local, and private philanthropic funds to provide a seamless continuum of services to the children and families it serves. However, to achieve these ends the organization has had to assume undue administrative burdens. For instance, the lack of alignment between grant periods means that it faces an almost continuous reporting cycle to remain in compliance with its various funding streams. Furthermore, the funding relationships with several agencies result in the "piling on" of rules and related compliance burdens.[8] To comply with all the rules, the organization must maintain as many as forty different data systems—that cannot "talk" to one another—in order to accommodate the reporting requirements and privacy rules of each separate program.

The costs of these efforts may not be readily apparent to the clients of Neighborhood Centers because, like other high-performance, high-capacity organizations, it has dedicated considerable time and resources to navigating and smoothing these disjointed funding streams. This situation reveals the irony of delivering scaled solutions within a fragmented system. A diverse funding portfolio not only allows scaled organizations to do *more* to serve a wider geographic area and provide a greater array of services; it also promotes organizational financial sustainability and gives them the latitude to address the multiple dimensions of need their clients face. However, this very breadth and diversity generates redundancies and inefficiencies that can divert resources away from an organization's mission.

The federal government can begin to remedy these systemic shortcomings by aligning data and reporting systems and requirements across programs and, where possible, across agencies. Reducing the number of data systems required for multiprogram providers and standardizing the way programs define terms or ask for relevant information would provide immediate savings in administrative costs. Moreover, organizations like Neighborhood Centers could gain additional efficiencies, and perhaps increase the quantity or quality of services further, if they could integrate, or "blend," data across programs to monitor the impacts of various investments at the family and community levels.

In addition to new efficiencies at the federal level, many of which could be implemented immediately without congressional action, states and localities can take measures to improve their own systems and service delivery networks. The Work Support Strategies initiative described in chapter 6 was formed to overcome high costs and inefficiencies in program delivery at the state and local levels. Although it is a voluntary program, the federal government could seed or reward system improvements to encourage their wider adoption. It could also require states and localities to adopt successful strategies in order to be eligible for other competitive funding (see "Bringing It Together" below). Doing so would create efficiency gains at multiple levels of government. Fewer program dollars, whether state or local, would be wasted by outdated and duplicative administrative structures, while more integrated and efficient systems could ease access to services for low-income households.

Building on these streamlined systems and networks, policymakers and funders at all levels should explicitly *promote high-performance organizations.* As noted earlier, despite its more than 100 years of service and its highly professional and regionally scaled administrative model, Neighborhood Centers is still subject to the same federal reporting requirements as much smaller, single-service organizations. But for this and other multiservice, multijurisdictional organizations, those requirements pile on top of one another in complicated and sometimes conflicting ways. Moreover, some federal programs even place limits on salaries for their grantees' top management personnel, such that executives at a $275 million nonprofit like Neighborhood Centers are subject to the same caps as those at grantees just a small fraction of its size.

These burdens reflect not just programmatic fragmentation but also the highly risk-averse nature of federal grant making generally. Sister Lillian Murphy and Janet Falk of Mercy Housing noted:

> Cautiousness on the part of government programs (at federal, state, and local levels) has led to separate regulations and rules that are designed for the one percent (or fewer) who might abuse the system, rather than the 99 percent who are in compliance. This model may be a good system to manage risk, but it is not a good system for getting to scale.[9]

Encouraging scale through true service integration—"breaking down the silos"—has a long, and somewhat disappointing, history at the federal level. The Congressional Research Service (CRS) documented a dozen different federal efforts from 1968 to 2004, including both enacted policies and legislative/administrative proposals, that aimed to facilitate integrated management and coordination of programs across agencies and jurisdictions. Most of these policies and programs relied on state and local governments to implement them by working with block grants, carrying out demonstration projects, or applying for specific waivers. CRS found that the efforts suffered from insufficient up-front investment, vague programmatic direction, limited administrative authority, and lack of tracking for accountability.[10] This track record suggests that the practical, legal, and political hurdles to effectively blending funding across multiple federal programs for greater flexibility remain high.

Short of full integration, however, the federal government could take meaningful steps toward rewarding scale in the nonprofit sector. One sensible and valuable move would be to recognize high-capacity organizations that are generating successful outcomes for their clients and reduce the reporting burdens they face. In essence, those organizations could be granted the opportunity to propose *their own* reporting protocols—format, timing, measures—to federal officials in the departments with which they interact. The federal government could require the same basic information, but could allow nonprofits to organize that information in ways that reduce duplication and administrative burdens, and that enable them to plan, evaluate, and improve their performance efficiently.

One can see the outlines of this direction in the Obama administration's 2013 budget proposal to enter into up to $200 million worth of "performance partnership pilots" with state and local governments around strategies to help disconnected youth and revitalize distressed neighborhoods. Those pilots would allow states and localities to blend funding across multiple federal programs in order to enhance cost effectiveness and outcomes. The proposal identifies simplifying reporting requirements and reducing administrative burdens as key steps that federal agencies could take to help states and localities deliver better results.[11]

Although focusing on reducing the reporting burdens of scaled non-profits would be somewhat narrower than the "blended funding" strategies that the performance partnership proposal envisions, reducing such burdens might also have wider applicability by focusing on the nonprofit delivery agents themselves, rather than intermediary state and local governments. The federal government could identify scaled, high-performance organizations by characteristics such as long-run financial stability, leadership experience and track record, positive independent evaluations of program delivery efficiency and efficacy, existence of internal planning and evaluation personnel and tracking of key program and client metrics, organizational "market share," and competitive advantages in their marketplace. It could designate an independent board of experts to award such organizational designations.

However, efforts to move to scale should not overlook the need to ground policy responses in the context of the local community. Another hallmark of high-performance organizations is the ability—to paraphrase Neighborhood Centers executive director Angela Blanchard—to scale what can be scaled but keep local what needs to be local. Organizations like Neighborhood Centers, Ways to Work, and IFF (formerly the Illinois Facilities Fund) have found ways to create efficiencies through scale while addressing the diverse and shifting needs of different places. Neighborhood Centers has centralized its finance and technology functions for greater efficiency while investing in local staff and intensive data-gathering efforts at each neighborhood site. IFF, as its service area has expanded to include states other than Illinois, has opened regional offices while retaining most back-office functions in its Chicago headquarters. Ways to Work has centralized lending services and program management software but has established partnerships with a network of existing providers to provide lending services in communities across the country.

Yet aligning systems and recognizing the role of existing high performers cannot ameliorate all of the effects of fragmentation. In some cases, the best path forward will be to *support smart consolidation*—a critical strategy for nonprofit organizations, public agencies, and suburban jurisdictions themselves.

The experience of Neighborhood Centers in navigating an array of relationships with other local nonprofits underscores another challenge particular to the nonprofit sector: not all nonprofits are able to make it to scale on their own. Just as government programs are often fragmented or duplicative, redundancies and inefficiencies exist in the nonprofit sector as well. The key to overcoming them is to create scaled and integrated solutions at the regional level. David La Piana argued that the problem is not necessarily too many nonprofits:

> A better conceptualization of the problem here is not the duplication of services, but the duplication of service provider infrastructures. Each organization employs an executive director, recruits a board of directors, and backs an administrative structure. Each also likely struggles to support information systems, human resource management, and budgeting and accounting processes. Merging organizations to combine their infrastructures often makes sense.[12]

However, La Piana said that formal mergers are not the only solution for nonprofits seeking greater efficiency and scale. Other options include management service organizations and joint venture corporations. In the former model, a group of nonprofits centralize administrative services by creating a legally separate corporation. The latter model uses the same structure but combines programs rather than administrative functions. In both cases, the organizations remain separate entities.[13]

Examining options to improve efficiencies and reduce replication among nonprofits often takes resources and capacity that organizations do not have. And they may require one-time fees to carry out the necessary restructuring. Although some funders specifically fund these types of efforts, philanthropy could do more to encourage and support organizational assessments along these lines, as well as fund strategic alliances and mergers.

A focus on the nonprofit sector should not, however, distract from the fact that federal, state, and local policies can also provide essential pathways to scaled solutions in metropolitan areas. For instance, even though housing markets are fundamentally metropolitan in nature, the Housing Choice Vouchers (HCVs) program is administered by several independent public housing authorities (PHAs) in each market, and 2,400 nationwide. Each PHA accepts applications, maintains waiting lists, certifies eligibility, collects data, and conducts briefings and inspections. The quality of these functions in many agencies is quite low. And while vouchers are technically portable across PHAs, the process of moving to a different PHA jurisdiction is administratively burdensome. Instead, as Bruce Katz and Margery Turner proposed, the Department of Housing and Urban Development (HUD) should shift governance of the voucher program to one organization or consortium for each metropolitan area through a competitive process. This would go a long way toward making the voucher program more sensitive to the affordable housing needs of both city and suburban low-income households, while reducing program costs and increasing program efficiency.[14]

Finally, overcoming the challenges of fragmentation in suburbia may require rethinking the number of suburban jurisdictions within a region. States have the authority to regulate land use, including the incorporation of municipalities. Thus, they have the power to discourage the proliferation of small suburban jurisdictions that cannot handle service challenges that arise as populations change over time. Ohio's Local Government Innovation Fund (LGIF) represents one promising model of a state taking the lead in assessing whether it makes sense for smaller municipalities to try to meet growing service needs on their own. However, just as with nonprofits, this strategic assessment process requires resources for planning and action before greater efficiencies and cost savings are realized. More states could incorporate this model into their own land use and planning approaches to not only reduce the proliferation of new jurisdictions but also repair existing fragmentation.

Promoting Collaboration and Integration

Backing organizations that can operate at the scale needed across metropolitan areas is clearly essential for confronting suburban poverty. Yet not all places will have the available public, private, or nonprofit vehicles for scaled delivery of services across the full range of issues that their populations and communities face.

For that reason, places must also get their existing actors to work better together, across jurisdictional and program lines. The collaborative approaches highlighted in the previous chapter have all found ways to overcome fragmentation—and the redundancies and gaps in capacity and resources that can arise from a fragmented system—to create crosscutting and effectively scaled solutions. Learning from their experiences, government officials and funders can support the implementation of such strategies by taking steps to:

—identify and reduce barriers to integration and collaboration,

—explicitly reward integrated and collaborative approaches, and

—catalyze regional capacity.

To advance these types of approaches in the near term, agencies must first *identify and reduce barriers* to integration and collaboration. Collaboratives trying to engage with existing programs encounter a lack of clarity in regulatory language and a tendency for agencies (or their proxies, like contract technical assistance providers) to narrowly interpret rules and regulations. They often assume that if rules do not explicitly *endorse* interjurisdictional entities, then such entities must be prohibited. This, too, reflects the risk-averse nature of federal grant making, to which Murphy and Falk referred.

In the Chicago suburbs, the collaboratives that initially formed to address the housing crisis encountered several obstacles to obtaining government funding. Although they attracted millions of dollars of investment in the years since they formed, each application, whether for federal, state, or local funds, required them to invest significant time and resources to overcome funding systems not designed for municipal collaboratives.

In the case of the West Cook County Housing Collaborative, because IFF played the role of coordinator, the collaborative was able to avoid the fragmented Neighborhood Stabilization Program funding that occurred in south Cook County (described in chapter 5). As a registered nonprofit and community development financial institution (CDFI), IFF managed the funds for the collaborative and acted as developer for the projects. However, this dual role created difficulties when it came time to apply for Community Development Block Grant (CDBG) Disaster Recovery funding. The Illinois Department of Commerce and Economic Opportunity expressed concern about a conflict of interest if IFF were to act as both coordinator and developer. It took eight months of negotiation to come to an agreement: IFF would serve as coordinator, drawing on its in-house expertise to evaluate and select outside developers, but would not act as the developer itself. Thus, though structured differently, each collaborative encountered challenges and delays in navigating the multiple levels of bureaucracy involved in securing government funding.

Rather than forcing collaborative entities across the country to repeatedly negotiate their rules, federal agencies—and their state and county counterparts—should acknowledge interjurisdictional collaboratives as qualified entities for relevant programs. At the federal level, the Office of Management and Budget should order a comprehensive, top-to-bottom review of programs to identify barriers to local collaboration—administrative, regulatory, and statutory—and recommend potential solutions. For instance, while HOME program dollars can go to a collaborative entity that contains both entitlement and nonentitlement communities, CDBG dollars cannot. This regulation blocks the flow of program dollars to suburban communities struggling with unprecedented growth in their poor populations. State and county agencies should follow suit, building on clarifications from the federal level to make their own program adjustments.

In addition to clarifying what is allowable within the terms of existing funding streams, government and philanthropic funders should *explicitly reward collaborative and integrated approaches*, to support existing efforts and encourage the adoption of these models in other regions.

In many instances, policymakers can create incentives for integration and collaboration within existing funding streams. For instance, federal programs could offer additional points to applications from entities pursuing collaborative strategies. Moreover, federal agencies could allow collaborative entities to incur administrative expenses as part of those programs (a common stumbling block in efforts to build collaborative resources and capacity).

States and counties can also do more to help eliminate fragmentation. Where local governance is highly fragmented, as it is in the Northeast and Midwest, they can create incentives for collaboration across jurisdictions—up to and including the merger of municipalities—either through existing funding streams or by carving out program dollars specific to those efforts. In Illinois, the governor signaled support for multijurisdictional collaborations by dedicating line-item funding to reward collaborative efforts that promote neighborhood stabilization efforts. Cook County's CDBG plan similarly encourages municipal collaboration, and the attorney general of Illinois authorized $70 million in National Foreclosure Settlement dollars to reward "sustainable, collaborative efforts in targeted areas," including neighboring municipalities.[15]

Ohio's LGIF provides much-needed financial support to analyze and pursue those endeavors.

Counties, councils of governments (COGs), and metropolitan planning organizations (MPOs), which operate at a more effective scale for addressing the scope of growing poverty, also have a clear role to play. The new Cook County administration has supported the suburban collaboratives outside of Chicago by awarding programmatic dollars and funding capacity development in the COG that houses the Southland collaborative.

However, not all counties, COGs, or MPOs are equally positioned to address the shifting geography of poverty—whether due to differences in capacity, resources, governance structure, the administration's priorities, or political will. In some cases, these entities may actually inhibit efforts to implement more scaled and collaborative approaches to fighting poverty and promoting opportunity. Existing networks like the National League of Cities and the National Association of Counties could provide the information and technical assistance necessary to educate municipal and county leaders about the shifting makeup and needs of their community, share best practices, and engage leadership on efforts to create and support more scaled and integrated solutions.

Philanthropic funders can also support and reward these solutions. In fact, they are a critical source of support that can *catalyze regional capacity in suburbia*. In the Chicago suburbs, the Chicago Community Trust and the Grand Victoria Foundation provided seed funding for the collaboratives and continue to support their coordinators and key intermediaries. Those are especially critical sources of support given the difficulty these groups have had collecting administrative fees from the government funding they attract. For the Road Map Project, the Seattle Foundation not only helped fund the formation of the project with other philanthropic partners in the region but also offered office space to the newly formed Community Center for Education Results. A combination of national and community foundations partnered with a handful of other agencies and intermediaries in both the Bay Area and the Denver region to support the development of affordable housing near transit lines.

While perhaps ill-suited to providing long-term core support for such initiatives, the strategic advantage of flexible philanthropic funding is its ability to catalyze innovative strategies and leverage additional funding. By seeding and supporting collaborative regional models, philanthropy can undergird the expansion of capacity and programmatic infrastructure often missing in suburbs struggling with rising poverty.

Funding Strategically and Flexibly

As organizations and regions across the country work to implement more scaled and collaborative solutions, funding remains a challenge. Scaled interventions require a diverse set of public and private funding sources and must demonstrate results. Yet while funders' expectations of efficiency and impact have risen, the legacy systems still in place often hamper those very innovations. To adapt to the contemporary realities of regionalizing poverty and limited resources, policymakers and private funders should:

—commit to enterprise-level funding,

—promote strategic tools that leverage public and private funds, and

—develop and maintain consistent, comparable data sources.

For many of the innovative and strategic funding models we have highlighted, the challenges and barriers to implementation stem from their novelty, the fragmentation and inflexibility of traditional funding sources, and their market-oriented approaches.

Negotiating and structuring enterprise-level investment often takes a significant amount of time and resources on the front end. If private investors and policymakers were to explicitly *commit to enterprise-level funding*, whether by offering increased flexibility among existing program funds or by tailoring new sources of funding accordingly, organizations and jurisdictions would have an incentive to think creatively and efficiently.

In the case of the Mortgage Resolution Fund (MRF), government acted as the upfront enterprise-level investor, with the Illinois Housing Development Authority (IHDA) agreeing to provide funds from the federal Hardest Hit Program in the form of a no-recourse, interest-free loan. That initial investment made it possible to implement the MRF model, with the Treasury Department, IHDA, and MRF agreeing on measurable targets for neighborhood stabilization. However, it took more than nine months for MRF to negotiate the program structure and agreement with IHDA and the Treasury Department. For the better part of a year, therefore, the mortgages MRF had targeted as likely to succeed under their approach to modification continued to age, in some cases missing the optimal window for restructuring to keep homeowners in their homes.

MRF faced another setback to implementation between closing with IHDA and the Treasury Department in November 2011 to the purchase of its first pool of mortgages in May 2012. Namely, in February 2012 the federal government and forty-nine state attorneys general reached a $25 billion settlement agreement with five of the nation's largest loan servicers over the scandal involving robo-signing of mortgage arrears and foreclosure documents. The market for the nonperforming loans MRF planned to acquire dried up as major sellers of nonperforming loans waited for the outcome of the settlement and for new rules to emerge. It took several months for the market to respond to these changes, meaning that once again the profile of the pool of delinquent properties shifted. Once the market began operating again, the pool contained more loans that had been delinquent for longer periods of time (more than 180 days), potentially limiting MRF's ability to find candidates that would help meet the program's goal of a 60 percent loan modification rate.[16]

MRF's experiences underscore a challenge inherent in any of the emerging enterprise-level, market-oriented strategies discussed here. The focus on outcomes as opposed to a narrowly prescribed set of administrative rules is central to the innovation and potential gains these approaches promise. The design of these strategies, however, takes time to get right and can leave organizations vulnerable to fluctuations in the market as well as disruptions caused by legal or government action. Enterprise-level funding must provide upfront planning time and support to structure such projects appropriately, as well as build in mechanisms for periodic assessment and recalibration to make sure interventions remain on track to meet agreed-upon goals.

To expand flexible and diversified funding sources, policymakers and funders should also *promote strategic tools that leverage public and private funds*. For instance, by testing new social impact investment vehicles, public and private funders can identify their appropriate structure and application.

Some of these vehicles are emerging from new government initiatives. The U.S. Department of Labor's Pay for Success program, discussed in chapter 6, represents a promising model for how federal agencies can use targeted pilots to support social impact financing. This approach could be replicated in other agencies. Another promising federal funding model is the Social Innovation Fund (SIF), launched in 2009 under the Edward M. Kennedy Serve America Act. Recognizing the innovative approach of the national capital region's Venture Philanthropy Partners (VPP), SIF awarded VPP $4 million in 2010 to create youthCONNECT—a collaboration of government, private philanthropy, nonprofits, and evaluators that targets efforts to improve opportunities for low-income youth aged

14 to 24. The award required a dollar-for-dollar match from VPP and further leveraged matching funds from other collaborators for a total initial investment of $13 million. In addition to leveraging private capital, SIF works with high-performing regional intermediaries—like VPP, Mile High United Way, United Way of Greater Cincinnati, and Twin Cities Strive—that make investments based on local needs.

Beyond government and philanthropic financing for more flexible and outcome-oriented models, private sector resources remain central to these approaches. The Community Reinvestment Act (CRA) provides an additional opportunity to spur private investments in social impact vehicles and help develop and target more resources to currently underserved communities and ill-equipped suburbs. Clarifying language on actions and investments that meet CRA goals, and potentially broadening the geographic definition of where activities may be targeted, could encourage the investment of private capital and diversify financial sector support beyond tried-and-true areas like affordable housing. Precedents for such adjustments exist: similar rule changes were made temporarily to support the deployment of Neighborhood Stabilization Program funds and related activities in areas hard hit by the foreclosure crisis.

Recognizing the potential risks of market-based approaches, Jeffrey Liebman observed that these types of models, and social impact bonds in particular, may be "a better fit for programs that offer supplemental services that could be terminated without disrupting clients' lives too much, rather than for 'core' services" like the basic operations of charter schools, child care centers, or prisons.[17] And because unforeseen disruptions can arise, flexible financing models must also have strategies for adapting to delays, changing market conditions, and falling short of key results benchmarks. In the case of social impact bonds, that may mean having a plan for what to do if initial financing collapses or a service provider fails to meet expectations.[18]

Above all, effective outcome-based, impact-oriented investments demand clear and accurate baselines and consistent tracking of targeted metrics. Their long-term success will thus depend on the ability of policymakers, funders, nonprofits, and the research community to *develop and maintain consistent, comparable data sources*. Maintaining modern systems for data collection and reporting is an essential role for government at all levels. At the federal level, the U.S. Census Bureau provides invaluable data resources, such as the annual American Community Survey, on key demographic and economic indicators. However, the relatively new Supplemental Poverty Measure—which provides a more comprehensive and nuanced look at economic hardship, including estimates of the poverty-alleviation impact of key federal programs like the EITC and SNAP—is not available below the state level. Although adapting the Supplemental Poverty Measure to produce substate estimates would be a complex process, it could significantly improve the ways in which regions approach and evaluate poverty alleviation.

Beyond the Census Bureau, the quality, detail, and geographic scope of publicly available data sets vary widely from agency to agency and program to program and can make the evaluation of community dynamics and program impacts difficult. For instance, tracking the uptake of safety net services like SNAP and unemployment insurance in the nation's largest metropolitan areas following the recession was hindered because not all states compile or report those data using consistent geographic boundaries (for example, counties).[19] While there may be programmatic or local reasons for using specially drawn boundaries, for the sake of public data reporting and comparisons, agencies should agree to make data available for a standard set of substate geographies.

But data and metrics are not an end in themselves. Nonprofit organizations and the research community also have a critical role to play in interpreting and evaluating publicly available data sets and indicators to assess the progress and impact of targeted interventions. Seidman posited that although "too great a focus on metrics can disadvantage the small (including the rural), the new and difficult to achieve, and things that take a long time to accomplish, the pressure to demonstrate impact suggests the value of developing strategies to overcome these concerns."[20] The federal government could spur the better use of data for assessing and improving metropolitan opportunity, as described below.

Setting the Stage for Success

The welfare reform debates of the late 1990s reflected a new consensus that the best antipoverty program is a job. But preparing people for and connecting them to jobs requires strategies that operate at the scale of the labor market. To modernize the U.S. approach to alleviating poverty and promoting opportunity, public policies must better engage with housing dynamics, transportation needs, service networks, and economic development at the regional level. Keeping decisions around these issues in separate silos risks recreating in suburbia the kinds of concentrated disadvantage that have become entrenched in so many urban centers throughout the country.

Many regional planning strategies across the country have made noteworthy strides in linking up decisions around housing, transportation, and jobs. But rarely is equitable development a first-order goal of these efforts. Without an explicit focus on the outcomes for low-income people and places, these models may fail to ameliorate the effects of regionalizing poverty in the long run. As Margaret Weir noted, "Indeed, many of the regional reform ideas that have been put into place in recent years have either been indifferent to low-income communities or have actually harmed them."[21]

However, building a more efficient, integrated, and flexible system for addressing regionwide poverty does not in itself guarantee that suburbs will receive the resources, capacity, and programming they need. The diversity of suburbia—from distressed to rapidly growing places, and from small towns to large counties—is reflected in the varying ability of suburban jurisdictions to absorb new resources. Living Cities defined *capital absorption capacity* as the "ability of communities to make effective use of capital to provide needed goods and services to underserved communities" and noted that "understanding the overall ecosystem (the interplay of the actors and functions that produces an environment for community investment) in a particular community is just as important as identifying the specific actors that are present or absent in that community."[22] Without adequate assessment and intentional action, coupled with clear signals and incentives from government and philanthropic sources, funding and other types of support will continue to flow down well-trodden paths to institutions and communities already equipped to compete for and readily disburse those resources. Ensuring that an improved system functions for an entire metropolitan area—and does not overlook pockets of need or merely shift resources from one part of a region to another—requires not only concerted efforts to increase the absorption capabilities of lagging suburban jurisdictions but also an understanding of how to balance the needs within varied and changing regions.

Subregional collaborations can help to align efforts around particular issues and articulate and elevate the needs and concerns of demographically and economically similar suburban enclaves within regions. However, there must also be mechanisms and structures that connect those efforts to a larger regional frame to ensure balanced development that will benefit the metropolitan area as a whole.

Where does the responsibility lie for connecting subregional needs and strategies at the regional scale? Who should facilitate the cross-cutting, regional interventions that will position metropolitan areas for success in the long run? David Erickson, Ian Galloway, and Naomi Cytron of the Federal Reserve Bank of San Francisco called this actor the "quarterback." They noted that in many communities, leadership on these issues has emerged from "unlikely places: schools, churches, charities, clinics, and elsewhere," and proposed:

> It would be the job of the quarterback to identify and build on those areas of leadership and strength, as well as to build capacity in the gaps. In that sense, the quarterback is really a facilitator who brings out the strengths of service providers and leaders in the community. . . . The work of the quarterback is a process and not a single idea or program. It is based on the latticework that the community development industry developed during the past 40 years, but it expands the scope dramatically to bring in new players, new sources of capital, and new ideas.[23]

In fact, regional quarterbacks have already emerged to spearhead and support innovations currently under way, and in many cases intermediaries have been uniquely positioned to step into this role. Often CDFIs—like IFF or the Low Income Investment Fund (LIIF), with in-house financial and development capabilities—can pivot to engage in broader community development efforts, helping to build capacity and facilitate planning. Other intermediaries, like the Metropolitan Mayors Caucus and the Metropolitan Planning Council in the Chicago area, have provided critical technical assistance and support to resource- and capacity-strapped suburbs, and have provided a regional perspective for integrated development strategies. Depending on the region, the quarterback may be a single entity or a coalition of regional actors bringing their skill sets together. Regardless, as government support likely declines in coming years, metropolitan areas will need strong intermediaries to facilitate the blending of multiple funding streams and to address capacity and resource gaps.

However, not all metropolitan areas are home to high-performing institutions of the caliber needed to provide that kind of leadership. Thus, the question remains how to develop and support more advanced intermediaries that can successfully step into the role of regional quarterback. The strategies and recommendations outlined above (and summarized in box 7-1) would facilitate smarter responses to the challenges of poverty at the regional scale. Yet a bolder, longer-term vision is needed, too.

Box 7-1. Near-Term Steps to Build a Better System for Confronting Poverty and Place

To support existing models of scaled, collaborative, and strategically funded solutions that address poverty and promote opportunity in metropolitan America, and to enable broader adoption of effective strategies, policymakers, practitioners, and funders should adopt reforms that adhere to the following tenets.

Getting to scale means taking steps to:
—improve systems and networks,
—promote high-performance organizations, and
—support smart consolidation.

Promoting collaboration and integration requires strategies that:
—identify and reduce barriers to integration and collaboration,
—reward integrated and collaborative approaches, and
—catalyze regional capacity.

Funding strategically and flexibly means that funders and practitioners should:
—commit to enterprise-level funding,
—promote strategic tools that leverage public and private funds,
—develop and maintain consistent, comparable data sources.

Finally, to set the stage for the successful implementation of each of these tenets in regions across the country, policymakers, practitioners, and funders must commit to:
—regional planning strategies that prioritize and promote equitable development,
—building capacity in places where it does not exist to ensure that struggling suburbs are poised to absorb and implement resources,
—strategies that engage and promote the regional intermediaries or "quarterbacks" who can help coordinate interventions across jurisdictions and policy silos.

Bringing It Together

Government and nonprofits can do many smart things to make the current system of place-based antipoverty policies work better for urban and suburban communities alike. Modest changes can lead to greater scale, enhanced collaboration, and more strategic use of resources within the basic contours of the system known today. And more communities and families could access the supports they need to find new economic opportunity and overcome poverty.

Still, implementing those solutions would fall woefully short of addressing the true scale of the challenge. Too few resources exist to address poverty community by community. Political and organizational forces continue to favor single-issue, top-down tactics over comprehensive, bottom-up approaches. Financial capacity, expertise, and public will are altogether absent in many of the places that now need them most. The American arsenal of "poverty and place" programs is no match for the global and local forces that are constantly reshaping metropolitan labor and housing markets.

Of course, these same issues have plagued the response to urban poverty for many years. Inner-city communities have not exactly thrived under a siloed, underresourced system that still leaves many individuals and families isolated from economic and educational opportunities. But now that suburban poverty is the norm in America, it is time to rethink how $82 billion a year in federal place-based antipoverty spending could work much better for more people and more places.

Although it would be ideal to start with a blank slate—and in fact, many suburban communities facing growing poverty today resemble that blank slate—the politics are complicated, to say the least. These funding streams are deeply embedded within separate cabinet agencies and congressional committees, and many are backed by powerful interest groups unlikely to yield ground for the sake of improving efficiency or effectiveness. More affirmatively, as chapter 6 demonstrated, innovative organizations across the country have the potential to transform the system from the inside out. The nation needs a new paradigm for alleviating poverty and promoting opportunity in metropolitan America that augments the power of those innovators and makes their approaches the norm rather than the exception.

To advance that paradigm, we should embrace three elements implicit in a series of recent initiatives that have yet to "break through" to the federal antipoverty apparatus: catalyzing reform, integrating by example, and elevating regional action.

Some competitive grant programs, particularly in the educational arena, are *catalyzing reforms* at the state and local levels by providing flexible, leveraged resources geared toward outcomes rather than outputs. The Department of Education's Race to the Top program is perhaps the best known of these efforts. States that adopted a list of key performance-focused educational reforms—most notably, the new Common Core Standards—became eligible for a portion of the program's $4.35 billion to support strategies for improving student achievement. The subsequent Race to the Top District program provided similar incentives to school districts to embrace rigorous evaluation and data systems in exchange for the opportunity to compete for flexible funds aimed at personalizing classroom learning to narrow achievement gaps. This bottom-up model is evident in other national contexts, such as the United Kingdom's City Deals, which streamline central government investments and provide added flexibility to cities that commit to plans and reforms designed to jump-start local economic growth.[24]

More federal policy efforts are *integrating by example* by attempting to cut across traditional agency lines and thereby promote integrated solutions at multiple levels of the system. For instance, HUD implemented the Sustainable Communities Initiative regional planning grants, but it worked closely with the Department of Transportation and the Environmental Protection Agency through the Sustainable Communities Partnership to coordinate those grants with existing federal investments in infrastructure, facilities, and services. Similarly, HUD and the Department of Education worked to ensure that their respective neighborhood-focused programs (Choice Neighborhoods and Promise Neighborhoods) encouraged on-the-ground coordination in low-income communities eligible for both investments.

In addition to the Sustainable Communities Initiative, federal policies in areas such as economic and workforce development and homeland security are *elevating regional action*, in recognition of the importance of regional coordination in tackling problems at the scale of the economy. Federal transportation policy was arguably the first arena to elevate regional action by creating metropolitan planning organizations in the 1960s and subsequently strengthening those organizations in the 1990s. In the 2000s, the Department of Labor's Workforce Innovation in Regional Economic Development (WIRED) program provided support to self-defined economic regions to integrate public workforce, higher education, and private initiatives in support of regionally competitive industry clusters. Today, the Federal Emergency Management Agency's Urban Areas Security Initiative allocates funding to enhance preparedness in the nation's largest metropolitan areas that are also at highest risk for a terrorist attack. And the Department of Energy, the Small Business Administration, and the Department of Commerce have invested in a series of programs in regional innovation clusters to enhance economic growth. In short, many parts of the federal policy apparatus outside place-based poverty programs are getting "regional religion."

These three elements—catalyzing reform, integrating by example, and elevating regional action—inform our proposal for a new Metropolitan Opportunity Challenge (box 7-2) to reinvent place-based

Box 7-2. Metropolitan Opportunity Challenge: A Proposal for Long-Term Systemic Change

To lay the foundation for a twenty-first-century antipoverty policy and practice framework that addresses poverty and opportunity at the regional level, we propose launching the Metropolitan Opportunity Challenge.

The Challenge would award federal funding totaling $4 billion to states through a competitive application process based on their proposals to increase access to opportunity for low-income residents and places through scaled, collaborative, and flexibly funded solutions.

Whom would it fund?

Successful applicants would detail how they would use the award to *spark state-level reforms* and *support tailored metro-level strategies*. The programs they design would help low-income people in a diverse array of places in their regions overcome barriers to opportunity (for example, related to training, transportation, health, housing).

How would it work?

The Challenge funding stream would *coordinate federal efforts* across agencies including HUD, Labor, Education, and Health and Human Services. It would offer incentives for states and regions to *blend mainstream funding* beyond Challenge dollars to address regional realities. A portion of the Challenge grant could be used to *fund for success*, rewarding states and regions that meet identified benchmarks within certain periods of implementation. The Challenge would support efforts to *deploy data strategically* and *grow metropolitan capacity*.

How would it be funded?

To assemble the initial pool of dollars, agencies would *redeploy existing federal place-based resources*, like those outlined in chapter 5. Repurposing just 5 percent of the current budget dedicated to addressing poverty and place could yield the proposed $4 billion dollar investment in the Challenge. Like the Department of Education's Race to the Top, the Challenge would *use limited resources to transform the field* by offering organizations and state and local governments incentives to reinvent approaches to regional poverty and opportunity, and to *leverage new resources* to address those challenges.

antipoverty strategy. This competitive federal funding stream would focus on increasing access to the opportunities and resources critical to the economic success of low-income families and communities throughout metropolitan areas, whether in cities or suburbs. By promoting the types of reforms we have detailed here and giving regions the flexibility to implement scaled-but-local strategies for enhancing opportunity across their diverse array of localities, the Metropolitan Opportunity Challenge would:

—*Spark state-level reforms.* Like Race to the Top, the Metropolitan Opportunity Challenge would (in the first instance) be a competitive grant program for states. To be eligible, states would be required to have adopted key reforms that streamline access to work supports for low-income individuals and families. For instance, the program could require eligible states to have implemented (and/or provide resources to help them implement) automated eligibility determinations and data sharing among SNAP, Temporary Assistance for Needy Families (TANF), Medicaid/CHIP, and child care programs. Such reforms are particularly meaningful for ensuring that eligible families throughout metropolitan areas gain access to those supports, given challenges around proximity and stigma that may limit take-up in suburban jurisdictions.

Choosing to fund states rather than metropolitan entities directly is not without potential pitfalls. States have often proven indifferent or hostile to metropolitan concerns, given the historical predominance of rural interests in state legislatures. This is slowly changing, however, as even traditionally rural states continue to accumulate economic and political power in their urban centers.[25] States remain critical to smart metro-level strategies, moreover, given their powers in policy areas such as transportation, education, housing, and skills training.[26] And as Race to the Top showed, new resources can encourage state-local collaboration on traditionally divisive issues. An additional hurdle in the Metropolitan Opportunity Challenge may come in the form of multistate regions, for which states would be required to devise joint strategies for promoting cross-border opportunity. Notwithstanding these potential difficulties, designing the challenge in this way would bring states to the table early to gain their cooperation in committing to long-term strategies for their metropolitan areas, while catalyzing system reforms that ultimately matter greatly for suburbs.

—*Support tailored metro-level strategies.* While states would be the primary grantees for the Metropolitan Opportunity Challenge, they would use the money in metropolitan areas to improve access to opportunity for low-income residents. As part of the application process, states—ideally jointly with metropolitan actors—would articulate how the Metropolitan Opportunity Challenge would provide enterprise-level funding to capable regional entities to implement strategies tailored to their places. They would be required to demonstrate scaled delivery plans, collaborative and integrated approaches, and strategic and flexible funding. The metropolitan-level strategies could focus on measurable outcomes that are judged to be most important for the economic advancement of lower-income populations in that metropolitan region, taking into account the diversity of community types in a region and their varying needs and assets. The goals of these interventions could include, among others, locating more affordable housing near good jobs or high-quality schools, stimulating economic development along key corridors that span distressed urban and suburban communities, scaling the delivery of social and health services to reach underserved areas, or coordinating the provision of workforce training and child care to help more adults prepare for in-demand careers.

The Metropolitan Opportunity Challenge would be agnostic about what type of entity carries out the strategy in any given state or metropolitan area—a nonprofit, a CDFI, a government agency, a metropolitan planning organization, or a consortium thereof—but would require states to demonstrate that those entities had the scale, expertise, and market understanding to tackle the strategy from a metropolitan perspective. In addition, the geography of the intervention could be regional or subregional, and applicants would be judged on how well that geography aligns with the issues identified, and the degree to which it promotes scaled delivery. Similar to the Race to the Top program, later rounds could provide federal funding directly to entities at the metropolitan level, but engaging states as grantees in at least the first round would be critical for gaining buy-in and leveraging their contributions to regional capacity over the long term.

—Bend "mainstream" funding. Funding for the Metropolitan Opportunity Challenge would give states and metropolitan areas the motivation and financial cushion to undertake new, tailored strategies. More than that, however, the challenge resources would obligate states and regions to bend existing place-based programs toward those new strategies. For instance, a state might propose to grant Metropolitan Opportunity Challenge dollars to a metropolitan area in order to increase the availability of high-quality schools in struggling suburban communities, and to increase the availability of affordable housing in suburban communities with good schools. While those dollars might provide the capital needed to establish new charter schools, attract high-quality staff to existing schools, or provide enhanced housing mobility counseling for low-income families, the state and metropolitan area would also be expected to align larger, existing funding flows such as Title I, the Low Income Housing Tax Credit, and the Housing Choice Vouchers program. Economic development strategies supported through the Metropolitan Opportunity Challenge could leverage significant state and local incentives dedicated to job attraction and retention in struggling areas. Applications for the Challenge would outline how each strategy would harness complementary federal, state, and local resources. Applicants would also be expected to detail what additional flexibility they would seek from federal agencies through waiver processes to enable policy and spending coordination. Ideally, the Challenge would encourage such resource alignment via systemic state- and metro-level reforms.

—*Fund for success.* The program could embrace the spirit of the growing Pay for Success movement by conditioning a portion of the funding on how well the strategies improved metropolitan access to opportunity. Because the aim of the Metropolitan Opportunity Challenge would be to enhance the long-term economic mobility of individuals and families in metropolitan areas through a range of strategies, it might not readily attract private capital focused on shorter-run government savings. However, while the bulk of challenge dollars would fund the design and implementation of access to opportunity strategies, "bonus" funding could be reserved for states that meet intermediate targets stipulated in the application process, such as measurable increases in low-income households' geographic access to employment via affordable transportation; children in voucher households attending well-performing schools; eligible families gaining access to subsidized nutritional assistance; or low-income individuals seeing a primary care physician on a regular basis. And by providing flexible, enterprise-level funding, the Challenge dollars would enable regions and states to think and act with a longer-term perspective, thereby avoiding the administrative burdens and narrow rule-making that erode the effectiveness of much program-level funding.

—*Deploy data strategically.* To measure gains in access to opportunity objectively, the Metropolitan Opportunity Challenge should incorporate funding for rigorous program evaluation and data sharing. Many of the data sets analyzed for this book and the Brookings Institution's Metropolitan Opportunity Series could prove useful for establishing strategy baselines and performance tracking. The federal government could engage philanthropy and the private sector to establish and support a common data platform to evaluate the progress of Metropolitan Opportunity Challenge participants and to stimulate similar efforts to improve access to opportunity in other metropolitan areas.

—*Grow metropolitan capacity*. The Metropolitan Opportunity Challenge would be designed not only to stimulate new metro-level thinking and action around access to opportunity but also to grow stronger networks of intermediaries and supporting institutions working at a regional scale. In some metropolitan areas, those entities (like Neighborhood Centers in Houston or IFF in the Midwest) might already exist. In others, the challenge could motivate new cross-sector, multijurisdictional partnerships. It could also attract new high performers to regions with limited existing capacity, in the way that the Department of Education's Charter Schools Program has encouraged the spread of high-performing charter management organizations to new markets. In keeping with the challenge aspect of the program, and similar to promising new efforts like SIF and the Investing in Innovation (i3) program, the Metropolitan Opportunity Challenge should require states and metropolitan areas to leverage the federal funds with matching dollars from the private and philanthropic sectors. It could thus motivate more national and regional philanthropies to move their grant making focus from neighborhoods and cities to regions. The Metropolitan Opportunity Challenge could also be separated into planning and implementation grant rounds, with planning grants allowing more regions time to assemble and test plans, and to attract or build the capacity of regional entities to carry out the plans.

—*Coordinate federal efforts*. Because Metropolitan Opportunity Challenge grants could incorporate interventions across policy areas, coordinated federal leadership would be needed to design and judge applications and to align existing federal resources and authorities behind the metropolitan strategies. The Departments of Housing and Urban Development, Education, Health and Human Services, and Labor operate the largest number of place-based programs identified in chapter 5 and should jointly administer the program under a special Metropolitan Opportunity Partnership. That partnership could in turn consult with other agencies whose investments could influence access to opportunity strategies, such as the Departments of Transportation, Commerce, and Justice. While interagency collaboration is not the most natural act in Washington, we believe that the benefits of aligning resources and rules behind the Metropolitan Opportunity Challenge strategies—as demonstrated through the Sustainable Communities Partnership—would outweigh the inevitable but manageable bureaucratic costs.

—*Redeploy existing place-based federal resources.* We propose that 5 percent of the existing $82 billion in annual federal place-based antipoverty funding—$4 billion—be redirected to the Metropolitan Opportunity Challenge. This is similar to the amount appropriated through the 2009 stimulus for Race to the Top, and a smaller share of total place-based program spending than Race to the Top represented as a share of the Department of Education's discretionary budget at the time. Exactly which programs should be trimmed to support the $4 billion program should be studied further, though it is notable that the Obama administration has already proposed (and in other cases acceded to) cuts in long-standing place-based programs such as CDBG, HOME, and the Community Services Block Grant. As the fiscal climate and divided government in Washington place further downward pressure on antipoverty spending, the Metropolitan Opportunity Challenge could represent an "escape valve" for repurposing additional cuts into a bolder, bottom-up approach to enhancing mobility at the regional scale of the economy.

—*Use limited resources to transform the field.* Admittedly, repurposing 5 percent of what we have termed a legacy system of policies and programs will not be sufficient to reimagine and reinvent antipoverty strategies for an age of suburban poverty. At the same time, the Race to the Top program had a truly transformative effect on state and local education reform with less than 1 percent of the total annual spending on K–12 education in the United States. Moreover, states and metropolitan areas supported by the Metropolitan Opportunity Challenge would be required to yoke existing place-based funding to these new regional efforts, boosting the program's true share well above 5 percent.

—*Leverage new resources.* The implementation of the Affordable Care Act (ACA) suggests that reinventing place-based policies is not necessarily a zero-sum game. Beyond the major provisions extending Medicaid eligibility and subsidizing households' purchase of private insurance through state health exchanges, the ACA made significant new investments in health care service access points for lower-income populations. The new Community Health Center Fund is providing $11 billion over a five-year period to expand health center capacity in medically underserved areas. The Prevention and Public Health Fund is spending $15 billion over a ten-year period to support programs for early detection and treatment of chronic diseases, and Medicaid is providing states with enhanced matching funds to provide preventive care services. Accountable care organizations, which coordinate care for Medicare beneficiaries and may under ACA share in the savings from serving them more efficiently and effectively, could eventually serve larger low-income patient populations and invest upstream in other social and educational services to generate better health outcomes.[27] Viewed strategically, the ACA can do more than just inject new dollars into lower-income places; it can fundamentally integrate health policy into a broader antipoverty agenda by targeting the so-called social determinants of health. Smart states and regions could use the Metropolitan Opportunity Challenge to make the most of those new opportunities as well.

Conclusion

Poverty is a hardship regardless of where one lives. Poor families strain to put enough food on the table, keep the lights on, and find decent-paying jobs, whether they live in Pittsburgh, Pennsylvania, or Pittsburg, California.

Confronting suburban poverty in America means confronting the common issues that affect city, suburban, and rural individuals and families with inadequate income, job and educational opportunities, and housing or health care. That means building metropolitan economies that create not just more jobs, but better jobs that are accessible to a growing and diversifying American workforce. And it means recommitting to income supports that can make up the yawning gap between wages and prices for families struggling to get ahead.

Place intersects with poverty in ways that can ease or exacerbate its challenges. Good schools, good jobs, good housing, and good services are not distributed equally across the American landscape. Places thus determine whether poor families have access to the tools, resources, and opportunities that can set them on a path to greater economic stability. That is why the rapid rise of poverty in suburbs in the 2000s, and the fact that suburbs now house more than half of our nation's metropolitan poor, should occasion a serious reassessment of how the United States combats poverty in place.

Throughout this book, we have detailed the complex array of factors that have contributed to poverty's suburbanization, as well as the implications of such rapid and significant change. Some of this shift resulted from very intentional public policies that sought to deconcentrate urban poverty and open up residential opportunities in suburbs for low-income families. As we have shown, however, being poor in a suburb is not always better, or always worse, than being poor in an inner city. It just brings with it a different set of challenges that public policy has yet to fully engage.

Therein lies the urgency. Decades of misguided public policy and mammoth economic and social shifts have devastated many of this nation's inner cities. Generations of individuals and families living in those communities—and American society as a whole—paid a terrible price. Concentrated urban poverty remains a huge problem today, one that is commanding new attention from education and housing reformers focused on breaking poverty's intergenerational grip on those neighborhoods. Yet suburban poverty remains something of a no-man's land for federal policy and local practice, even as it has overtaken urban poverty in magnitude. By neglecting its rise, the country stands to repeat the mistakes of the past and consign millions of new families and communities to a grim future. Business as usual threatens to further entrench the very dynamics that have fueled rising inequality within and across regions.

But the solution is not to play a zero-sum game, shifting resources from poor urban to poor suburban communities. The sum is simply not large enough. Today's landscape of poverty demands new policies and practices that confront barriers to opportunity not just at the community level, but at the regional scale of the economy. Only then can poverty alleviation become more productive, stretching limited dollars to help more people in more places.

Fortunately, we do not have to invent such an approach from scratch. As has always been true in America, entrepreneurial leaders and organizations are innovating to solve these challenges from the bottom up. They are embracing scale, collaborating and integrating across places and programs and deploying funding strategically and flexibly. As a nation, we now need to move their efforts from the exception to the norm. A series of near-term reforms outlined in this chapter, from streamlined reporting requirements to incentives for collaboration to enhanced private sector leverage, could immediately ease the implementation and replication of these smarter strategies and help more low-income people access economic and social opportunities in their regions.

Even those reforms, however, will fail to transform the legacy system America has created for confronting poverty in place. Thus, we call for a Metropolitan Opportunity Challenge, a new effort to help regions and states organize their strategies and resources to wrest that $1.20 in value from each $0.80 of resources. The Metropolitan Opportunity Challenge would greatly accelerate the progress that some regions are already making. Rather than introducing more top-down programs, the Challenge could catalyze solutions to the diverse problems of poverty in metropolitan areas from the bottom up, and help reinvent antipoverty policy from the inside out.

Even as he helped to invent America's antipoverty policies nearly a half-century ago, President Lyndon Johnson appreciated the need to adapt those strategies over time. In his Great Society speech at the University of Michigan's commencement in May 1964, Johnson laid out a vision for the next fifty years: an end to poverty and racial injustice, particularly in cities; preservation of America's natural resources; and educational opportunity for all. Yet the Great Society, he remarked, "is not a safe harbor, a resting place, a final objective, a finished work. It is a challenge constantly renewed."[28]

President Johnson could scarcely have imagined what the next fifty years would bring. But he undoubtedly would have expected that by 2014 the nation's approach to building a stronger American society would be quite different from that in 1964. The suburbanization of poverty renews that original challenge and demands modernized responses. The next fifty years may not eradicate American poverty once and for all, but they must unleash new and adaptive systems that build and rebuild ladders of opportunity for poor families and communities nationwide.

Notes

Chapter One

1. Alex Schafran, "The Cities of Carquinez," *Urbanist*, no. 514 (June 2012).

2. Eros Hoagland, "As Program Moves to the Suburbs, Tensions Follow," *New York Times*, August 8, 2008.

3. Chris Schildt, "Diversity Didn't Cause the Foreclosure Crisis," *Urbanist*, no. 514 (June 2012).

4. Peter Dreier, John Mollenkopf, and Todd Swanstrom, *Place Matters: Metropolitics for the Twenty-First Century* (University Press of Kansas, 2001).

5. Elliot Liebow, *Tally's Corner: A Study of Negro Streetcorner Men* (New York: Back Bay Books, 1967); Department of Labor Office of Research and Planning, "The Negro Family: The Case for National Action" (Washington, 1965).

6. Ken Auletta, *The Underclass* (New York: Random House, 1982); Nicholas Lemann, "The Origins of the Underclass," *Atlantic Monthly* 256 (June 1986): 31–55; Erol R. Ricketts and Isabel V. Sawhill, "Defining and Measuring the Underclass," *Journal of Policy Analysis and Management* 7 (February 1988): 316–25.

7. William Julius Wilson, *When Work Disappears: The New World of the Urban Poor* (New York: Knopf, 1996); Wilson went on to explore the impact of both structural and cultural influences on poor black families in urban neighborhoods in *More Than Just Race: Being Black and Poor in the Inner City* (New York: Norton, 2009).

8. William Julius Wilson, *The Truly Disadvantaged: The Inner City, the Underclass, and Public Policy* (University of Chicago Press, 1987).

9. Douglas Massey and Nancy Denton, *American Apartheid: Segregation and the Making of the Underclass* (Harvard University Press, 1993).

10. Paul A. Jargowsky, *Poverty and Place: Ghettos, Barrios, and the American City* (New York: Russell Sage Foundation, 1997); Paul A. Jargowsky and Mary Jo Bane, "Ghetto Poverty: Basic Questions," in *Inner-City Poverty in the United States*, edited by Laurence E. Lynn and Michael T. McGeary (Washington: National Academy of Sciences Press, 1990), pp. 16–67; John D. Kasarda, "Inner-City Concentrated Poverty and Neighborhood Distress: 1970–1990," *Housing Policy Debate* 4, no. 3 (1993): 253–302; Paul A. Jargowsky, "Stunning Progress, Hidden Problems: The Dramatic Decline of Concentrated Poverty in the 1990s,"Metropolitan Policy Program Report (Washington: Brookings Institution, 2003); Rolf Pendall and others, "A Lost Decade: Neighborhood Poverty and the Urban Crisis of the 2000s" (Washington: Joint Center for Political and Economic Studies, 2011); Elizabeth Kneebone, Carey Nadeau, and Alan Berube, "The Re-Emergence of Concentrated Poverty:

Metropolitan Trends in the 2000s," Metropolitan Opportunity Series 23 (Washington: Brookings Institution, 2011).

11. Roberto G. Quercia and George C. Galster, "Threshold Effects and Neighborhood Change," *Journal of Planning and Education Research* 20, no. 2 (2000): 146–62; George C. Galster, "The Mechanism(s) of Neighborhood Effects: Theory, Evidence, and Policy Implications," lecture, St. Andrews University, Scotland, February 4–5, 2010.

12. David A. Cotter, "Poor People in Poor Places: Local Opportunity Structures and Household Poverty," *Rural Sociology* 67, no. 4 (December 2002): 534–35; Ann R. Tickamyer and Cynthia M. Duncan, "Poverty and Opportunity Structure in Rural America," *Annual Review of Sociology* 16 (1990): 67–86.

13. Janet M. Fitchen, *Poverty in Rural America: A Case Study* (Boulder, Colo.: Westview Press, 1981).

14. Cynthia M. Duncan, *Worlds Apart: Why Poverty Persists in Rural America* (Yale University Press, 2000).

15. Marybeth J. Mattingly, Kenneth M. Johnson, and Andrew Schaefer, "More Poor Kids in More Poor Places: Children Increasingly Live Where Poverty Persists" (Durham, N.H.: Carsey Institute, 2011); Kathleen K. Miller and Bruce A. Weber, "Persistent Poverty across the Urban-Rural Continuum," Working Paper 03-01 (Washington: Rural Poverty Research Center, 2003); Duncan, *Worlds Apart.*

16. Bernadette Hanlon, John Rennie Short, and Thomas J. Vicino, *Cities and Suburbs: New Metropolitan Realities in the U.S.* (New York: Routledge, 2010), p. 51.

17. Kenneth T. Jackson, *Crabgrass Frontier: The Suburbanization of the United States* (Oxford University Press, 1985), p. 236.

18. Ibid., pp. 237–38.

19. William H. Lucy and David L. Phillips, *Confronting Suburban Decline: Strategic Planning for Metropolitan Renewal* (Washington: Island Press, 2000), p. 3.

20. Dolores Hayden, *Building Suburbia: Green Fields and Urban Growth, 1820–2000* (New York: Pantheon Books, 2003).

21. Kevin M. Kruse and Thomas J. Sugrue, eds., *The New Suburban History* (University of Chicago Press, 2006), p. 6.

22. Hanlon, Short, and Vicino, *Cities and Suburbs*; Kruse and Sugrue, *New Suburban History.*

23. Kruse and Sugrue, *New Suburban History*; Lucy and Phillips, *Confronting Suburban Decline.*

24. National Center for Environmental Economics, "The United States Experience with Economic Incentives for Protecting the Environment" (Washington: U.S. Environmental Protection Agency, 2001).

25. Hayden, *Building Suburbia.*

26. Hanlon, Short, and Vicino, *Cities and Suburbs.*

27. Jackson, *Crabgrass Frontier.*

28. Andres Duany, Elizabeth Plater-Zyberk, and Jeff Speck, *Suburban Nation: The Rise of Sprawl and the Decline of the American Dream* (New York: North Point Press, 2000), p. 130.

29. Hayden, *Building Suburbia*; Dreier, Mollenkopf, and Swanstrom, *Place Matters*; Lucy and Phillips, *Confronting Suburban Decline.*

30. Charles Tilly, *Durable Inequality* (University of California Press, 1998).

31. Jonathan Rothwell and Douglas Massey, "Density Zoning and Class Segregation in U.S. Metropolitan Areas," *Social Science Quarterly* 91 (2010): 1123–43. As Rolf Pendall and his colleagues have documented, the application of these policies has varied considerably across places. While policies in metropolitan areas in the West tend to focus more on the pace and shape of development, midwestern and northeastern metropolitan areas are more likely to use land-use regulation for exclusionary purposes. Rolf Pendall, Robert Puentes, and Jonathan Martin, "From Traditional to Reformed: A Review of the Land Use Regulations in the Nation's 50 Largest Metropolitan Areas," Metropolitan Policy Program Report (Washington: Brookings Institution, 2006).

32. Hayden, *Building Suburbia*; Kruse and Sugrue, *New Suburban History*.

33. Myron Orfield, *Metropolitics: A Regional Agenda for Community and Stability* (Washington: Brookings Press, 1997); Myron Orfield, *American Metropolitics: The New Suburban Reality* (Washington: Brookings Press, 2002); Lucy and Phillips, *Confronting Suburban Decline*; Kathryn W. Hexter and others, "Revitalizing Distressed Older Suburbs" (Washington: Urban Institute, 2011); Robert Puentes and Myron Orfield, "Valuing America's First Suburbs: A Policy Agenda for Older Suburbs in the Midwest," Metropolitan Policy Program Report (Washington: Brookings Institution, 2002); Robert Puentes and David Warren, "One-Fifth of America: A Comprehensive Guide to America's First Suburbs," Metropolitan Policy Program Report (Washington: Brookings Institution, 2006); Hanlon, Short, and Vicino, *Cities and Suburbs*.

34. Lucy and Phillips, *Confronting Suburban Decline*.

35. Puentes and Orfield, "Valuing America's First Suburbs."

36. See also Puentes and Warren, "One-Fifth of America."

37. Orfield, *American Metropolitics*.

Chapter Two

1. See, for example, Sylvia Allegretto, "Basic Family Budgets: Working Families' Budgets Often Fail to Meet Living Expenses around the U.S." (Washington: Economic Policy Institute, 2005); Jared Bernstein, Chauna Brocht, and Maggie Spade-Aguilar, *How Much Is Enough? Basic Family Budgets for Working Families* (Washington: Economic Policy Institute, 2000); Gregory Acs and Pamela Loprest, "Who Are Low-Income Working Families?" Accessing the New Federalism Project 1 (Washington: Urban Institute, 2005).

2. Only one—McAllen, Texas—achieved a decrease in the suburban poverty rate, not because the poor population dropped but because it grew more slowly than the overall population.

3. We identify all suburban jurisdictions—including incorporated places (or, in the case of New England states, Minor Civil Divisions [MCDs]) and counties—with sufficient population to be included in the three-year ACS estimates (20,000). Using population-based allocation factors from the Missouri Data Center's MABLE/Geocorr application, we remove the municipalities/MCDs in our universe from their surrounding counties to produce "net county" estimates that avoid double-counting residents.

4. Elizabeth Kneebone, Carey Nadeau, and Alan Berube, "The Re-Emergence of Concentrated Poverty: Metropolitan Trends in the 2000s," Metropolitan Opportu-

nity Series 23 (Washington: Brookings Institution, 2011); and Brookings Institution analysis of 2006–10 ACS data.

5. George C. Galster, "The Mechanism(s) of Neighborhood Effects: Theory, Evidence, and Policy Implications," lecture, St. Andrews University, Scotland, February 4–5, 2010.

6. In keeping with broader trends in family formation, both cities and suburbs experienced a decline over the 2000s in the share of poor families headed by married couples (3.1 and 4.3 percentage points, respectively). At the same time, suburbs experienced a significant increase in poor households headed by single fathers and single mothers (0.9 and 1.5 percentage points, respectively). In contrast, poor households headed by women without children was the only category to experience a statistically significant increase in cities.

7. William H. Frey, "Melting Pot Cities and Suburbs: Racial and Ethnic Change in Metro America in the 2000s," Metropolitan Policy Program Report (Washington: Brookings Institution, 2011).

Chapter Three

1. Audrey Singer, Susan W. Hardwick, and Caroline B. Brettell, "Twenty-First Century Gateways: Immigrants in Suburban America" (Washington: Migration Policy Institute, April 2008) (www.migrationinformation.org/Feature/display.cfm?ID=680).

2. The strength of the relationship between unemployment and poverty has fluctuated over time. Through the 1970s the effect of rising unemployment on poverty was large. Though it weakened in the 1980s, it has since strengthened, and Blank found that poverty remained very responsive to the economic cycle in the 2000s. See Rebecca Blank, "Economic Change and the Structure of Opportunity for Less-Skilled Workers," in *Changing Poverty, Changing Policies*, edited by Maria Cancian and Sheldon H. Danziger (New York: Russell Sage Press, 2009), pp. 63–91.

3. Emily Monea and Isabel Sawhill, "An Update to 'Simulating the Effect of the "Great Recession" on Poverty,'" Social Genome Project Research 20 (Washington: Brookings Institution, 2011).

4. National Bureau of Economic Research (NBER), "U.S. Business Cycle Expansions and Contractions" (Washington, 2010); Julie Hatch Maxfield, "Jobs in 2005: How Do They Compare to Their March 2001 Counterparts?" *Monthly Labor Review* 129, no. 7 (2006): 15–26.

5. David S. Langdon, Terence M. McMenamin, and Thomas J. Krolik, "U.S. Labor Market in 2001: Economy Enters a Recession," *Monthly Labor Review* 125, no. 2 (2002): 3–33.

6. Maxfield, "Jobs in 2005"; David Langdon, Rachel Krantz, and Michael Strople, "A Visual Essay: Post-Recession Trends in Nonfarm Employment and Related Economic Indicators," *Monthly Labor Review* 127, no. 9 (2004): 49–56.

7. NBER, "U.S. Business Cycle Expansions and Contractions."

8. Christopher J. Goodman and Steven M. Mance, "Employment Loss and the 2007–09 Recession: An Overview," *Monthly Labor Review* 134, no. 4 (2011): 3–12.

9. Megan M. Barker, "Manufacturing Employment Hard Hit during the 2007–09 Recession," *Monthly Labor Review* 134, no. 4 (2011): 28–33; Goodman and Mance, "Employment Loss and the 2007–09 Recession."

10. The Annual Social and Economic Supplement to the Current Population Survey (CPS) provides the historical estimates of the national poverty rate used in figure 3-1. The American Community Survey (ACS), which began releasing annual data in 2005, produces slightly different estimates than the CPS. For example, the CPS poverty rate for 2010 was 15.1 percent, whereas the ACS single-year estimate for 2010 was 15.3 percent. For a discussion of differences between the two surveys, see the U.S. Census Bureau online fact sheet (www.census.gov/hhes/www/poverty/about/datasources/factsheet.html).

11. Josh Bivens and John Irons, "A Feeble Recovery: The Fundamental Economic Weakness of the 2001–07 Expansion," Briefing Paper 214 (Washington: Economic Policy Institute, 2008).

12. Brookings Institution, "State of Metropolitan America Indicator Map," 2012 (www.brookings.edu/research/interactives/state-of-metropolitan-america-indicator-map).

13. Alan Berube and Elizabeth Kneebone, "Two Steps Back: City and Suburban Poverty Trends, 1999–2005," Metropolitan Policy Program Report (Washington: Brookings Institution, 2006).

14. Elizabeth Kneebone and Emily Garr, "March 2010: The Landscape of Recession: Unemployment and Safety Net Services across Urban and Suburban America," Metropolitan Opportunity Series 3 (Washington: Brookings Institution, 2010); Emily Garr, "March 2011: The Landscape of Recession: Unemployment and Safety Net Services across Urban and Suburban America," Metropolitan Opportunity Series 10 (Washington: Brookings Institution, 2011).

15. Kneebone and Garr, "March 2010: Landscape of Recession."

16. Elizabeth Kneebone, "Job Sprawl Stalls: The Great Recession and Metropolitan Employment Location," Metropolitan Policy Program Report (Washington: Brookings Institution, 2013).

17. U.S. Bureau of Labor Statistics, "A Profile of the Working Poor, 2010" (Washington, 2012).

18. Kneebone, "Job Sprawl Stalls."

19. Steven Raphael and Michael A. Stoll, "Job Sprawl and the Suburbanization of Poverty," Metropolitan Opportunity Series 4 (Washington: Brookings Institution, 2010).

20. Kneebone, "Job Sprawl Stalls."

21. National Employment Law Project, "The Low Wage Recovery and Growing Inequality" (New York, 2012).

22. C. Brett Lockard and Michael Wolf, "Occupational Employment Projections to 2020," Monthly Labor Review 135, no. 1 (2012): 84–108.

23. William H. Frey, "Population Growth in Metro America since 1980: Putting the Volatile 2000s in Perspective," State of Metropolitan America 47 (Washington: Brookings Institution, 2012), p. 5.

24. Maria Cancian and Deborah Reed, "Family Structure, Childbearing, and Parental Employment: Implications for the Level and Trend in Poverty," Focus 26, no. 2 (Madison, Wis.: Institute for Research on Poverty, 2009), pp. 21–26.

25. Brookings Institution, "State of Metropolitan America Indicator Map," 2012 (www.brookings.edu/ research/interactives/state-of-metropolitan-america-indicator-map).

26. Audrey Singer, Susan W. Hardwick, and Caroline Brettell, Twenty-First Century Gateways: Immigrant Incorporation in Suburban America (Washington: Brookings Press, 2008).

27. Roberto Suro, Jill H. Wilson, and Audrey Singer, "Immigration and Poverty in America's Suburbs," Metropolitan Opportunity Series 18 (Washington: Brookings Institution, 2011).

28. Counting the native-born children of poor immigrant parents as foreign born would generally point toward a higher contribution of immigration to suburban poverty growth. Although it is not possible to calculate that contribution across all suburbs given data limitations, an analysis of census microdata in the Seattle region suggests that, from 2000 to 2009, foreign-born individuals accounted for 19 percent of suburban poverty growth, and all individuals in foreign-born-headed families accounted for 32 percent of that growth. This analysis is based on the methodology presented in Paul A. Jargowsky and Karina Fortuny, "Decomposing the Impact of Immigration on Metropolitan Area Poverty Rates: 1980–2007," paper presented at the Annual Meeting of the Urban Affairs Association, March 12, 2010, Honolulu, Hawaii, and the Annual Research Meeting of the Association of Public Policy Analysis and Management, November 5, 2010, Boston, Massachusetts.

29. Author interviews with local officials.

30. Thomas Bier, "Moving Up, Filtering Down: Metropolitan Housing Dynamics and Public Policy," Metropolitan Policy Program Report (Washington: Brookings Institution, 2001).

31. Henry W. McGee Jr., "Seattle's Central District, 1990–2006: Integration or Displacement?" *Urban Lawyer* 39, no. 2 (2007): 167–236.

32. Brooke DeRenzis, "Population Dynamics in the District of Columbia since 2000," Metropolitan Policy Program Report (Washington: Brookings Institution, 2008).

33. See, for example, Lance Freeman, "Displacement or Succession? Residential Mobility in Gentrifying Neighborhoods," *Urban Affairs Review* 40, no. 4 (2005): 463–91; Philip Nyden, Emily Edlynn, and Julie Davis, "The Differential Impact of Gentrification on Communities in Chicago," prepared for the City of Chicago Commission on Human Relations by Loyola University Chicago Center for Research and Learning (2006).

34. Data on the number and type of subsidized households come from HUD's "A Picture of Subsidized Households" online database for 2000 and 2008. The counts represent occupied units for which HUD received forms HUD-50058 and HUD-50059 from public housing agencies and landlords; thus they do not necessarily reflect the entire stock of HUD housing. For instance, approximately 7 percent of public housing was vacant or held off the market as of December 2008. Of occupied units, HUD received tenant data for 96 percent of households. For Housing Choice Vouchers, 93 percent of units under contract were in use, and HUD received tenant data for 98 percent of such units.

35. Susan J. Popkin, Bruce Katz, Mary K. Cunningham, Karen Brown, Jeremy Gustafson, and Margery A. Turner, "A Decade of HOPE VI: Research Findings and Policy Challenges" (Washington: Urban Institute, 2004).

36. Xavier de Souza Briggs, Susan Popkin, and John Goering, *Moving to Opportunity: The Story of an American Experiment to Fight Ghetto Poverty* (New York: Oxford University Press, 2010).

37. Kenya Covington, Lance Freeman, and Michael Stoll, "The Suburbanization of Housing Choice Voucher Recipients," Metropolitan Opportunity Series 22 (Washington: Brookings Institution, 2011).

38. Ibid.

39. Brookings Institution analysis of "A Picture of Subsidized Households" data (see note 34).

40. Covington, Freeman, and Stoll, "The Suburbanization of Housing Choice Voucher Recipients."

41. All data on lending and foreclosures in the suburbs of the nation's 100 largest metropolitan areas come from Chris Schildt, Naomi Cytron, Elizabeth Kneebone, and Carolina Reid, "The Subprime Crisis in Suburbia: Exploring the Links between Foreclosures and Suburban Poverty" (San Francisco, Calif.: Federal Reserve Bank of San Francisco, 2013).

42. The correlation coefficient between foreclosure rates and change in suburban poverty rate in metropolitan areas from 2007 to 2010 was 0.68.

43. Brookings Institution analysis of U.S. Census Bureau building permits and population estimates data.

44. Public Advocates and Bay Area Legal Aid, "Policing Low-Income African American Families in Antioch: Racial Disparities in 'Community Action Team' Practices" (San Francisco, 2007); Brookings Institution analysis of U.S. Census Bureau data.

45. Kristin Perkins, "A Snapshot of Foreclosure in Contra Costa County" (Berkeley, Calif.: Center for Community Innovation, 2008).

46. Public Advocates, "Williams *v.* City of Antioch," October 26, 2011 (www.publicadvocates.org/williams-v-city-of-antioch).

Chapter Four

1. Alexandra Murphy, "The Social Organization of Black Suburban Poverty: An Ethnographic Community Study," PhD dissertation, Princeton University, 2012.

2. Harry J. Holzer and Michael Stoll, "Where Workers Go, Do Jobs Follow? Metropolitan Labor Markets in the U.S., 1990–2000," Metropolitan Policy Program Report (Washington: Brookings Institution, 2007).

3. Steven Raphael and Michael Stoll, "Job Sprawl and the Suburbanization of Poverty," Metropolitan Opportunity Series 4 (Washington: Brookings Institution, 2010), p. 15. This is consistent with earlier research from Holzer and Stoll, in "Where Workers Go, Do Jobs Follow?" where they observed that racial and ethnic minorities drove population growth in lower-income suburbs with weaker employment gains and lower access to well-paying jobs.

4. Kenya Covington, Lance Freeman, and Michael Stoll, "The Suburbanization of Housing Choice Voucher Recipients," Metropolitan Opportunity Series 22 (Washington: Brookings Institution, 2011).

5. Robert Hickey, Jeffrey Lubell, Peter Haas, and Stephanie Morse, "Losing Ground: The Struggle of Moderate-Income Households to Afford the Rising Costs of Housing and Transportation" (Washington: Center for Housing Policy and Center for Neighborhood Technology, 2012).

6. Commuting statistics come from internal tabulations of 2008 American Community Survey data on fifty-two large metropolitan areas and can be found on the Brookings "State of Metropolitan America" interactive indicator map

7. Matthew Fellowes, "From Poverty, Opportunity: Putting the Market to Work for Lower Income Families," Metropolitan Policy Program Report (Washington: Brookings Institution, 2006). Moreover, research by the Consumer Federation of America (CFA) found that low- and moderate-income households often pay premiums that consume a higher percentage of their household income, and "reflect disparate treatment and/or disparate impact." Steven Brobeck and J. Robert Hunter, "Lower-Income Households and the Auto Insurance Marketplace: Challenges and Opportunities" (Washington: Consumer Federation of America, January 2012) (www.consumerfed.org/news/450).

8. J. Robert Hunter, "GEICO Ties Insurance to Education, Occupation: Many Lower Income, Minority Consumers Pay Higher Prices" (Washington: Consumer Federation of America, 2006).

9. See, for example, Evelyn Blumenberg and Peter Haas, "The Transportation Needs and Behavior of Welfare Participants in Fresno County," U.S. FHWA Report FHWA/CA/OR-2001023 (San Jose, Calif: Mineta Transportation Institute, 2002); Robert Cervero, Juan Onèsimo Sandoval, and John Landis, "Transportation as a Stimulus of Welfare-to-Work: Private versus Public Mobility," Journal of Planning Education and Research 22, no. 1 (2002): 50–63.

10. Analysis of 2008 ACS data on the Brookings "State of Metropolitan America" interactive indicator map (www.brookings.edu/research/interactives/state-of-metropolitan-america-indicator-map).

11. Adie Tomer, Elizabeth Kneebone, Robert Puentes, and Alan Berube, "Missed Opportunity: Transit and Jobs in Metropolitan America," Metropolitan Opportunity Series 12 (Washington: Brookings Institution, 2011).

12. Ibid. Notably, coverage rates for subsidized households (whether voucher holders or those living in place-based projects) prove slightly higher in the suburbs (81 percent), but the share of jobs reachable in ninety minutes proves slightly lower (24 percent). Brookings Institution analysis of transit access and U.S. Department of Housing and Urban Development (HUD) data on the location of subsidized households.

13. Adie Tomer, "Transit Access and Zero-Vehicle Households," Metropolitan Infrastructure Initiative Series 21 (Washington: Brookings Institution, 2011).

14. Scott W. Allard, Out of Reach: Place, Poverty, and the New American Welfare State (Yale University Press, 2009).

15. As Allard and Roth observed, "Most social service programs are funded by federal, state, or local government, but delivered by community-based nonprofit organizations." Scott W. Allard and Benjamin Roth, "Strained Suburbs: The Social Service Challenges of Rising Suburban Poverty," Metropolitan Opportunity Series Report (Washington: Brookings Institution, 2010), p. 2. In some cases county and local governments also provide certain types of safety net programs. This section focuses on the nonprofit safety net in suburbia, but we return to a discussion of local government capacity in chapter 5.

16. Alexandra Murphy and Danielle Wallace, "Opportunities for Making Ends Meet and Upward Mobility: Differences in Organizational Deprivation across Urban and Suburban Poor Neighborhoods," Social Science Quarterly 91, no. 5 (2010): 1164–86.

17. Scott W. Allard, "Access to Social Services: The Changing Urban Geography of Poverty and Service Provision," Metropolitan Policy Program Report (Washington: Brookings Institution, 2004).

18. Margaret Weir, "Creating Justice for the Poor in the New Metropolis," in *Justice and the American Metropolis*, edited by Clarissa Hayward and Todd Swanstrom (University of Minnesota Press, 2011), p. 245.

19. Mario Small, *Unanticipated Gains: Origins of Network Inequality in Everyday Life* (Oxford University Press, 2009).

20. Allard and Roth, "Strained Suburbs."

21. Ibid., pp. 10–11. Allard and Roth note that IRS form 990 data on registered nonprofits do not fully reflect the extent to which providers registered in one county or municipality reach into surrounding areas, nor do 990 data capture nonprofits with budgets of less than $25,000 or small church-based programs that are not required to file tax-exempt status. But their findings are consistent with surveys and interviews suggesting that suburbs lack the capacity to adequately address shifting and rising needs.

22. Ibid., p. 8.

23. In 2012, LCSC served roughly 12,000 unduplicated clients, about 95 percent of whom reside in Lakewood (a community with a population of roughly 52,000 in 2010). Lakewood is not typical of suburban jurisdictions in the Cleveland area in that the city runs a Department of Human Services with divisions for early childhood, youth, and the elderly. However, they do not offer services for adults; thus the bulk of LCSC's clients are working-age residents.

24. Interview with Trish Rooney, Lakewood, Ohio, January 31, 2012.

25. Sarah Reckhow and Margaret Weir, "Building a Stronger Regional Safety Net: Philanthropy's Role," Metropolitan Opportunity Series 17 (Washington: Brookings Institution, 2011), p. 6.

26. Some providers in cities also serve suburbs, such as Families First in Atlanta, which is located in the city but operates satellite programs in a number of suburbs. The opposite also occurs; Gleaners Community Food Bank is located in the Detroit suburb of Oak Park but serves five counties in the region, including the city of Detroit.

27. Reckhow and Weir, "Building a Stronger Regional Safety Net," pp. 8–9.

28. See, for example, Nonprofit Finance Fund, "2012 State of the Nonprofit Sector Survey," April 2012 (www.nonprofitfinancefund.org/announcements/2012/state-of-the-nonprofit-sector-survey).

29. Allard and Roth, "Strained Suburbs," p. 1.

30. Ibid., p. 14.

31. See, for example, Elizabeth Kneebone and Emily Garr, "March 2010: The Landscape of Recession: Unemployment and Safety Net Services Across Urban and Suburban America," Metropolitan Opportunity Series 3 (Washington: Brookings Institution, 2010); and Emily Garr, "March 2011: The Landscape of Recession: Unemployment and Safety Net Services Across Urban and Suburban America," Metropolitan Opportunity Series 10 (Washington: Brookings Institution, 2011).

32. Brookings Institution analysis of 2010 ACS data on food stamp receipt by household poverty status.

33. Nonprofit Finance Fund, "2012 State of the Nonprofit Sector Survey."

34. Steven Lawrence, "Foundation Growth and Giving Estimates" (New York: Foundation Center, 2012).

34. Steven Lawrence, "Foundation Growth and Giving Estimates" (New York: Foundation Center, 2012).

35. Students in families with income below 130 percent of the federal poverty guidelines qualify for free lunch, while students whose family incomes are between 130 and 185 percent of the poverty line are eligible for reduced-price lunch. Brookings analysis of National Center for Education Statistics Common Core Data.

36. Brookings analysis of GreatSchools data.

37. Ingrid Gould Ellen and Keren Mertens Horn, "Do Federally Assisted Households Have Access to High Performing Schools?" (Washington: Poverty and Race Research Action Council, 2012).

38. California State Department of Education, Standardized Testing and Reporting (STAR) Results, 2011 (http://star.cde.ca.gov/star2011/).

39. Pennsylvania Department of Education, 2011–12 Pennsylvania System of School Assessment (PSSA) District results (www.education.state.pa.us/portal/server.pt/community/school_assessments/7442).

40. A number of suburban schools and school districts interviewed emphasized the importance of government grant and philanthropic dollars in helping to plug the gap between existing funding streams and the growing needs of the student body and community, particularly in light of an uneven local safety net. The administrative burden of competing for, administering, and reporting on such funding streams has led some school districts—such as Adams 14 and Mapleton Public Schools outside Denver, each of which strives to provide extensive wraparound services for students and often the broader community—to dedicate scarce resources to a staff grant writer. In other cases, like Lakewood High School, existing staff members take on these responsibilities in addition to their primary duties.

41. Allard and Roth, "Strained Suburbs"; Reckhow and Weir, "Building a Stronger Regional Safety Net."

42. Author interviews with regional and suburban service providers.

43. Alejandro Portes and Ruben G. Rumbaut, *Immigrant America: A Portrait* (University of California Press, 1990).

44. See, for example, University of Texas at Austin, "Crime on the Rise?" (www.utexas.edu/features/2008/crime).

45. Elizabeth Kneebone and Steven Raphael, "City and Suburban Crime Trends in Metropolitan America," Metropolitan Opportunity Series 16 (Washington: Brookings Institution, 2011).

46. That is not to say that some communities have not experienced upticks in crime in recent years, or that slower declines in suburban crime do not raise questions or concerns about future public safety trends. But increasing or persistent suburban crime rates likely reflect the strains of growth and urbanization in many suburbs, rather than increasing diversity, while resources remain stretched if not cut back, given continuing local fiscal woes. In this vein, Steven Levitt found that demographic shifts were not an important factor in the decline of violent crime in the 1990s, but the increase in the number of police was. He noted that while changes in the economy have little direct effect on crime trends, indirect effects likely emerge due to the impact on state and local budgets, which determine the number of police employed. See Steven Levitt, "Understanding Why Crime Fell in the 1990s: Four Factors that Explain the Decline and Six that Do Not," *Journal of Economic Perspectives* 18, no. 1 (2004): 163–90.

47. As noted in chapter 2, the 1,817 suburban jurisdictions we identify in the 100 largest metropolitan areas include incorporated places (or, in the New England states, Minor Civil Divisions [MCDs]) and counties with sufficient population to be included in the ACS (20,000). Using population-based allocation factors from Missouri Data Center's MABLE/Geocorr application, we remove the municipalities/MCDs in our universe from their surrounding counties to produce "net county" estimates that avoid double counting residents.

48. Robert E. Lang and Jennifer Lefurgy, *Boomburbs: The Rise of America's Accidental Cities* (Brookings Press, 2007).

Chapter Five

1. Susan Longworth, "Suburban Housing Collaboratives: A Case for Interjurisdictional Collaboration," *Profitwise News and Views* (Chicago: Community Development and Policy Studies Division of the Federal Reserve Bank of Chicago, 2011).

2. Woodstock Institute, "Chicago City and Regional Foreclosure Activity" (Chicago, 2010).

3. As described in chapter 6, HUD and new Cook County leadership eventually put their support behind the collaborative approaches developed in Chicago's suburbs.

4. For examples of the Obama administration's efforts to promote more integrated and comprehensive planning, see the Sustainable Communities Regional Planning Grant program, which "supports metropolitan and multijurisdictional planning efforts that integrate housing, land use, economic and workforce development, transportation, and infrastructure investments" and "places a priority on investing in partnerships, including nontraditional partnerships" (www.grants.gov/search/search.do?mode=VIEW&oppId=109013).

5. Dominic Tocci, "Multi-Town Collaboration Is Now an Imperative," Metropolitan Planning Council, November 22, 2011 (www.metroplanning.org/news-events/article/6279), p. 2.

6. President Lyndon B. Johnson, "Annual Message to the Congress on the State of the Union," January 8, 1964 (www.lbjlib.utexas.edu/johnson/archives.hom/speeches.hom/640108.asp).

7. Bruce Katz, "Neighborhoods of Choice and Connection: The Evolution of American Neighborhood Policy and What It Means for the United Kingdom," Metropolitan Policy Program Report (Washington: Brookings Institution, 2004).

8. See, for example, Sarah Reckhow and Margaret Weir, "Building a Stronger Regional Safety Net: Philanthropy's Role," Metropolitan Opportunity Series 17 (Washington: Brookings Institution, 2011); Pascale Joassart-Marcelli and Jennifer R. Wolch, "The Intrametropolitan Geography of Poverty and the Nonprofit Sector in Southern California," *Nonprofit and Voluntary Sector Quarterly* 32, no. 1 (2003): 70–96.

9. Alexander von Hoffman, "The Past, Present, and Future of Community Development in the United States," in *Investing in What Works for America's Communities: Essays on People, Place, and Purpose*, edited by Nancy Andrews and David Erickson (San Francisco: Federal Reserve Bank of San Francisco and Low Income Investment Fund, 2012), pp. 12–15.

10. Katz, "Neighborhoods of Choice and Connection."

12. The programs in this category provide resources to governments and non-profit organizations to promote the economic revitalization of lower-income neighborhoods; all programs explicitly target substate geographies for those resources. They exclude programs characterized by individual or family enrollment and those that do not have an explicit revitalization purpose (for example, public housing and project-based rental assistance).

13. For analysis of the effects of the CRA on home mortgage lending to low- and moderate-income communities, see Robert E. Litan, Nicolas Retsinas, Eric Belsky, and Susan White Haag, "The Community Reinvestment Act after Financial Modernization: A Final Report" (Washington: U.S. Department of the Treasury, 2001).

14. The programs in this category include several that are targeted to governments or nonprofit organizations that serve areas of high "need," such as those with large low-income populations. They exclude programs characterized by individual or family eligibility and enrollment, such as SNAP (food stamps), Medicaid, and Temporary Assistance for Needy Families (TANF).

15. See, for example, Scott Allard and Benjamin Roth, "Strained Suburbs: The Social Service Challenges of Rising Suburban Poverty," Metropolitan Opportunity Series Report (Washington: Brookings Institution, 2010). Research has also shown that people-based benefits like the Earned Income Tax Credit (EITC), a refundable tax credit that boosts earnings of low-income workers and their families, have a spatial impact in the form of local multiplier effects. However, as the high participation rate of the EITC suggests (roughly 80 percent of eligible filers claim the credit), there appear to be fewer spatial barriers to accessing the credit because it is claimed through filing an annual tax return. Instead, in this category of policies we focus on services and benefits that may prove accessible or inaccessible based on spatial proximity. See, for example, Caroline M. Sallee, "Economic Benefits of the Earned Income Tax Credit in Michigan" (East Lansing, Mich.: Anderson Economic Group, 2009); Dean Plueger and Amy O'Hara, "Earned Income Tax Credit TY2005 Participation Rate," presented at the 2009 IRS Research Conference (www.irs.gov/pub/irs-soi/09resconlowincome.pdf); Elizabeth Kneebone and Emily Garr, "Responding to the New Geography of Poverty: Metropolitan Trends in the Earned Income Tax Credit," Metropolitan Opportunity Series 9 (Washington: Brookings Institution, 2011).

16. These community types are defined in chapter 4.

17. See HUD's Community Planning and Development Program Formula Allocations for FY 2012 (http://portal.hud.gov/hudportal/HUD?src=/program_offices/comm_planning/about/budget/budget12).

18. Brookings Institution analysis of Census Bureau and Health Resources and Services Administration data.

19. HUD funded sixteen housing authorities under the Regional Opportunity Program, an initiative designed to encourage movement of voucher recipients away from high-poverty neighborhoods by counseling recipients on opportunities in lower-poverty communities. The program ended in 1999, though a handful of housing authorities continue to offer counseling services per court order. See Kenya Covington, Lance Freeman, and Michael Stoll, "The Suburbanization of Housing Choice Voucher Recipients," Metropolitan Opportunity Series 22 (Washington: Brookings Institution, 2011).

20. Joel A. C. Baum and Christine Oliver, "Toward an Institutional Ecology of Organizational Founding," *Academy of Management Journal* 39, no. 5 (October 1996): 1378–1427.

21. Allard and Roth, "Strained Suburbs."

22. Phil Oliff, Chris Mai, and Vincent Palacios, "States Continue to Feel Recession's Impact" (Washington: Center on Budget and Policy Priorities, 2012).

23. Author interview with Charlotte Ciancio, October 5, 2012.

Chapter Six

1. See "Montgomery County Community Partnerships Mission" (www.montgomerycountymd.gov/partnerships/contact/index.html).

2. Birgit Heitfeld, "Red Scarf Power" (www.citiscope.org/2010/red-scarf-power).

3. The Work Support Strategies project receives primary funding from the Ford Foundation.

4. See "Work Support Strategies: Streamlining Access, Strengthening Families," Urban Institute (www.urban.org/worksupport/North Carolina.cfm).

5. Chicago Metropolitan Agency for Planning, Metropolitan Mayors Caucus, Chicago Metropolitan Planning Council, "Supporting and Sustaining Interjurisdictional Collaboration for Housing and Community Development" (Chicago, 2012).

6. Susan Longworth, "Suburban Housing Collaboratives: A Case for Interjurisdictional Collaboration," *Profitwise News and Views* (Chicago: Community Development and Policy Studies Division of the Federal Reserve Bank of Chicago, 2011).

7. "Our Region" (www.roadmapproject.org/the-project/our-region).

8. Jeff Edmonson and Nancy Zimpher, "The New Civic Infrastructure: The 'How To' of Collective Impact and Getting a Better Social Return on Investment," *Community Investments* 24, no. 2 (2012): 10–13.

9. Two other multijurisdictional entities received Race to the Top awards alongside the Road Map Project: the Green River Regional Educational Cooperative, which is a multidistrict consortium in Kentucky, and Harmony Science Academy/Harmony Public Schools in Texas, which is a consortium of public charter schools that fall under the Harmony Schools umbrella but are located in multiple districts.

10. The projects funded in the TOAH Fund's first two years of existence were located in the cities of San Francisco, Oakland, and San Jose; however, the fund has since identified a number of suburban sites in its project development pipeline that will receive funding.

11. Sarah Reckhow and Margaret Weir, "Building a Stronger Regional Safety Net: Philanthropy's Role," Metropolitan Opportunity Series 17 (Washington: Brookings Institution, 2011).

12. The Hardest Hit Fund sent resources to the housing finance agencies in eighteen states (and the District of Columbia) with above-average unemployment rates and declines in home prices greater than 20 percent.

13. As of February 2013, MRF was in negotiations with the Ohio Housing Finance Agency, the U.S. Treasury, and a private commercial lender to leverage the Hardest Hit Fund in Ohio, also with a focus on properties in suburban clusters particularly affected by the foreclosure crisis.

14. Anthony Bugg-Levine, "Future of Community Development: How CDFIs Can Best Ride the Impact Investing Wave," in *Investing in What Works for America's Communities: Essays on People, Place, and Purpose*, edited by Nancy Andrews and David Erickson (San Francisco: Federal Reserve Bank of San Francisco and Low Income Investment Fund, 2012), pp. 152–53.

Chapter Seven

1. For instance, the new SparkPoint Center in Bay Point coordinates services for low-income clients across a range of service areas. See Eve Mitchell, "SparkPoint Center in Bay Point Provides a One-Stop Center for Social Services Programs," *Contra Costa Times*, July 3, 2012.

2. Congressional Budget Office, "Choices for Deficit Reduction" (Washington, 2012).

3. Pete Domenici and Alice Rivlin, "Restoring America's Future: Reviving the Economy, Cutting Spending and Debt, and Creating a Simple, Pro-Growth Tax System" (Washington: Bipartisan Policy Center, 2010); Alan Simpson and Erskine Bowles, "The National Commission on Fiscal Responsibility and Reform: The Moment of Truth" (Washington: White House, 2010).

4. Ellen Seidman, "Integration and Innovation in a Time of Stress: Doing the Best for People and Place," in *Investing in What Works for America's Communities: Essays on People, Place, and Purpose*, edited by Nancy Andrews and David Erickson (San Francisco: Federal Reserve Bank of San Francisco and Low Income Investment Fund, 2012), pp. 362–63.

5. Michael A. Pagano, Christopher W. Hoene, and Christiana McFarland, "City Fiscal Conditions in 2012" (Washington: National League of Cities, 2012). Note that 12 percent of cities surveyed increased funding for human services and 8 percent increased education funding.

6. On program effectiveness, see, for example, Jimmy Charite, Indivar Dutta-Gupta, and Chuck Marr, "Studies Show Earned Income Tax Credit Encourages Work and Success in School and Reduces Poverty" (Washington: Center on Budget and Policy Priorities, 2012).

7. Ben Hecht, "Community Development: Reflecting on What Works," *Stanford Social Innovation Review* blog, December 7, 2012.

8. For instance, the Head Start centers of Neighborhood Centers must navigate overlaps among performance standards promulgated by the U.S. Department of Health and Human Services, licensing requirements and health and safety standards from the Texas Department of Protective and Regulatory Services, nutritional standards from the U.S. Department of Agriculture, safety rules from the city of Houston, and additional credentialing standards from the National Association for the Education of Young Children.

9. Sister Lillian Murphy and Janet Falk, "Getting to Scale: The Need for a New Model in Housing and Community Development," in *Investing in What Works for America's Communities*, edited by Andrews and Erickson, p. 240.

10. Cheryl Vincent, "The 'Superwaiver' Proposal and Service Integration: A History of Federal Initiatives" (Washington: Congressional Research Service, 2005).

11. See Fiscal Year 2013 Budget of the U.S. Government, General Provisions Government-Wide (www.whitehouse.gov/sites/default/files/omb/budget/fy2013/assets/ggp.pdf).

12. David La Piana, "Merging Wisely," *Stanford Social Innovation Review* (Spring 2010): 28–33.

13. Ibid.

14. Bruce Katz and Margery Austin Turner, "Streamlining Housing Voucher Administration," Metropolitan Policy Program Report (Washington: Brookings Institution, 2013).

15. See "Request for Qualifications and Proposals: National Foreclosure Settlement Awards; Housing Counseling and Community Revitalization" (www.illinoisattorneygeneral.gov/consumers/settlementpdfs/ConfCall_Presentation2113.pdf).

16. Eventually the Federal Housing Administration (FHA) significantly increased its sale of nonperforming mortgages. In addition to national mortgage pools, FHA allowed jurisdictions to create subpools that aligned with their own neighborhood stabilization strategies. MRF joined with IHDA to create a carve-out of 324 FHA mortgages in the Chicago region and successfully bid on the subpool.

17. Jeffrey Liebman, "Social Impact Bonds: A Promising New Financing Model to Accelerate Social Innovation and Improve Government Performance" (Washington: Center for American Progress, 2011), p. 25.

18. Ibid.

19. Elizabeth Kneebone and Emily Garr, "March 2010: The Landscape of Recession: Unemployment and Safety Net Services Across Urban and Suburban America," Metropolitan Opportunity Series 3 (Washington: Brookings Institution, 2011).

20. Seidman, "Integration and Innovation in a Time of Stress," p. 370.

21. Margaret Weir, "Creating Justice for the Poor in the New Metropolis," in *Justice and the American Metropolis*, edited by Clarissa Hayward and Todd Swanstrom (University of Minnesota Press, 2011), pp. 237–56.

22. Living Cities, "The Capital Absorption Capacity of Places: A Self Assessment Tool" (New York, 2012), p. 2.

23. David Erickson, Ian Galloway, and Naomi Cytron, "Routinizing the Extraordinary," in *Investing in What Works for America's Communities*, edited by Andrews and Erickson, pp. 385, 405.

24. Rachel Smith and Joe Sarling, "Here's the Deal: Overview of the Wave 1 City Deals" (London: Centre for Cities, 2012).

25. A. G. Sulzberger, "Rural Legislators' Power Ebbs as Populations Shift," *New York Times*, June 2, 2011.

26. Bruce Katz and Jennifer Bradley, "Metro Connection," *Democracy* (Spring 2011): 53–63.

27. In Akron, Ohio, the Austen BioInnovation Institute has developed the concept of an Accountable Care Community, a collaborative, multi-institutional approach focused on health promotion, disease prevention, access to quality services, and health care delivery. It addresses the health outcomes of Summit County, Ohio, as a whole, rather than, in the case of an accountable care organization, a defined popula-

tion of health consumers. Austen BioInnovation Institute, "Healthier by Design: Creating Accountable Care Communities: A Framework for Engagement and Sustainability" (Akron, Ohio, 2012).

28. President Lyndon B. Johnson, "The Great Society," Address to University of Michigan, May 22, 1964.

Index